前 言 *PREFACE*

英国思想家培根说过：阅读使人深刻。阅读的真正目的是获取信息，开拓视野和陶冶情操。从语言学习的角度来说，学习语言若没有大量阅读就如隔靴搔痒，因为阅读中的语言是最丰富、最灵活、最具表现力、最符合生活情景的，同时读物中的情节、故事引人入胜，进而能充分调动读者的阅读兴趣，培养读者的文学修养，至此，语言的学习水到渠成。

"麦格希中英双语阅读文库"在世界范围内选材，涉及科普、社会文化、文学名著、传奇故事、成长励志等多个系列，充分满足英语学习者课外阅读之所需，在阅读中学习英语、提高能力。

◎难度适中

本套图书充分照顾读者的英语学习阶段和水平，从读者的阅读兴趣出发，以难易适中的英语语言为立足点，选材精心、编排合理。

◎精品荟萃

本套图书注重经典阅读与实用阅读并举。既包含国内外脍炙人口、耳熟能详的美文，又包含科普、人文、故事、励志类等多学科的精彩文章。

◎功能实用

本套图书充分体现了双语阅读的功能和优势，充分考虑到读者课外阅读的方便，超出核心词表的词汇均出现在使其意义明显的语境之中，并标注释义。

鉴于编者水平有限，凡不周之处，谬误之处，皆欢迎批评教正。

我们真心地希望本套图书承载的文化知识和英语阅读的策略对提高读者的英语著作欣赏水平和英语运用能力有所裨益。

丛书编委会

麦格希 **中英双语阅读文库**

古希腊神殿

世界新知馆 第4辑

麦格希中英双语阅读文库编委会●编

吉林出版集团股份有限公司

图书在版编目（CIP）数据

世界新知馆. 第4辑, 古希腊神殿 / 美国麦格劳-希尔教育集团主编；丁丽蓉, 吴鹏译；麦格希中英双语阅读文库编委会编. -- 2版. -- 长春：吉林出版集团股份有限公司, 2018.3

（麦格希中英双语阅读文库）

书名原文：Timed Readings Plus in Social Studies Book 9

ISBN 978-7-5581-4797-5

Ⅰ.①世… Ⅱ.①美… ②丁… ③吴… ④麦… Ⅲ.①英语—汉语—对照读物②社会科学—通俗读物 Ⅳ.①H319.4：C

中国版本图书馆CIP数据核字(2018)第046401号

世界新知馆　第4辑　古希腊神殿

编：	麦格希中英双语阅读文库编委会	
插　画：	齐　航　李延霞	
责任编辑：	沈丽娟	
封面设计：	冯冯翼	
开　本：	660mm×960mm　1/16	
字　数：	225千字	
印　张：	10	
版　次：	2018年3月第2版	
印　次：	2018年3月第1次印刷	

出　版：	吉林出版集团股份有限公司
发　行：	吉林出版集团外语教育有限公司
地　址：	长春市泰来街1825号
	邮编：130011
电　话：	总编办：0431-86012683
	发行部：0431-86012767　0431-86012826(Fax)
印　刷：	香河利华文化发展有限公司

ISBN 978-7-5581-4797-5　　定价：29.90元

Contents

1

The Ancient Greek Temple

The ancient Greeks *colonized* much of the ancient world, from one extreme of the Mediterranean Sea to the other. Much of the architecture of these once-thriving communities now can only be imagined. Mere fragments survived almost three thousand years of natural disasters and those caused by people. It is *apparent*,

古希腊神殿

古希腊人在古代开拓了大量的殖民地，从地中海的一端扩展到另一端。那些曾经繁盛一时的社会所兴建的建筑物，如今大部分都只能想象了。经历了近三千年所发生过的天灾人祸，留存下来的仅仅是残垣断片而已。然而，这些城市的建造者，显然都是才华出众的艺术家和

---

colonize v. 把……变为殖民地   apparent adj. 明显的

however, that the builders of these cities were talented artists and inventive engineers. One example of their abilities is the ancient Greek temple.

Initially little more than a room with a porch, the Greek temple evolved into a distinctive and majestic *edifice*. The typical structure included a rectangular enclosure encircled by a row of columns called a peristyle. The enclosure and columns rested on a low platform. They were covered by a pitched wood-and-tile roof. Except for the roof, temples were constructed from blocks of stone and featured brightly painted sculptural decorations.

At either end of the building, the slanting eaves of the roof and the horizontal lintel above the columns created a triangular gable, or *pediment*. The space inside the pediment was enriched with

富有创造力的工程师。古希腊神殿即是他们能力的一个见证。

最初的希腊神殿只是一个有门廊的宅屋，后来才逐渐演变成一座风格迥异、雄伟壮观的楼宇。神殿的典型结构称为周柱廊，即用一排柱廊环绕起来的矩形围护结构。围护结构和柱廊以一低台支撑，上覆盖木瓦坡屋顶。除了屋顶，神殿的其他部分都用大块石料砌成，以色调明快的雕刻装饰为特色。

在建筑的两端，坡屋顶的两个斜檐和柱廊上方的横梁构成了一个三角墙，或称山形墙。三角墙墙内空间装饰有纪念众神和展现希腊神话故事片

edifice *n.* 大厦；雄伟的建筑物　　　　　　pediment *n.* 山形墙

sculptures honoring the gods and illustrating *episodes* from Greek mythology. The columns were fluted, carved with long vertical ridges, and *surmounted* by decorative tops called capitals. The earliest temples were in the Doric style. The capitals of Doric columns resembled a rounded cushion. The Ionic-style columns were more slender than those in the Doric style, leading some art historians to describe the Ionic style as "feminine" and the Doric as "masculine." Ionic capitals are carved with a spiral, called a volute, in the shape of a ram's horn.

The most famous Greek temple is the Parthenon, in Athens. It was built in the fifth century B.C. and dedicated to Athena Parthenos, the goddess of wisdom. It is astonishing that this *exquisite* Doric temple exists at all. In ancient times, marble was taken from the

---

段的雕刻。圆柱上有凹槽，雕刻有长长的垂脊，顶上覆盖着的装饰物叫做柱顶。最早的神殿为多立克式。多立克式柱顶看上去似一个表面磨光的圆垫。爱奥尼克式圆柱比多立克式更细长，所以一些艺术历史学家将爱奥尼亚式称为"阴性"，将多立克式称为"阳性"。爱奥尼亚式柱顶雕刻有呈公羊角形状的螺旋，叫做盘涡形饰。

最著名的希腊神殿是位于雅典的帕特农神殿，建于公元前五世纪，用以供奉智慧女神雅典娜。令人惊讶的是这座精美的多立克式神殿居然完好保存至今。古时候，帕特农神殿的大理石常让人取走用于修建其他建

---

episode *n.* 插曲；事件　　　　　　surmount *v.* 置于（某物）顶端
exquisite *adj.* 精致的；高雅的

Parthenon for use in other buildings. It was converted at one point into a Christian church and then into an Islamic mosque, with much of the original decoration removed. In the seventeenth century, it was nearly destroyed, when gunpowder stored there exploded. Shortly thereafter many of the surviving sculptures were removed and placed on exhibition at the British Museum, in England. Air pollution and acid rain have damaged much of what remains of the structure. Today it gleams a brilliant white against the *azure* sky, its polychromed surfaces long since *scrubbed* clean by weather and damage.

筑。它曾一度改建成一座基督教堂，然后又改建成了伊斯兰清真寺，许多装饰品真迹流散异地。17世纪时，它差点因贮存于里面的火药爆炸而毁于一旦。不久后，许多渡过劫难的雕塑品被运送到英国，并陈列于大不列颠博物馆内，对公众展出。这座神殿遗址受到了空气污染和酸雨的破坏。如今，它在蔚蓝天空衬托下，辉映出耀眼的白色，色彩斑斓的表层已让长久以来的天气与人为因素给荡涤得一干二净了。

---

azure *adj.* 蔚蓝的   scrub *v.* 用力刷洗

2

The Greek Revival Style: Architecture for a New Nation

A country's monuments and public buildings are as much an expression of its ideals as its politics. The writers of the United States Constitution had found models for their ideals in Greek *democracy* and the republican government of ancient Rome. It is not surprising, therefore, that American *architects* also looked to Greece

希腊复兴式建筑：一个新国家的建筑艺术

一个国家的历史遗迹和公共建筑既可以体现它的政治，又可以展示它的理想。美国宪法的作者从希腊民主制度和古罗马共和政府体制中为他们的理想找到了榜样。所以，美国建筑师在为新国家蓬勃兴起的城市修建重要的建筑物时，也参照希腊和罗马建筑风格，这一点并不

---

democracy n. 民主政体   architect n. 建筑师

and Rome when they created important structures for the new nation's growing cities.

The neoclassical style, as it is known, reflected the traditions of both of those ancient civilizations. Buildings that copied particular features of Greek architecture were part of the Greek Revival movement. These features often include a porch front with columns topped by a *triangular* pediment. Houses in the Greek Revival style were often painted white in the mistaken belief that the Greek models had been made mostly from unpainted, shining white *marble*.

The Custom House, built in 1832 and located on Wall Street in

---

足为奇。

众所周知，新古典风格反映了那两种古文明的传统。建筑时效仿希腊建筑的某些特征是希腊复兴运动的一部分。这些特征一般包括一个前门廊，数根圆柱顶起的一面三角墙。某些人错误地认为，以前的希腊典范式建筑大都是由未涂色、亮白理石材建造而成，故希腊复兴式房屋通常漆成白色。

建于1832年，位于曼哈顿闹市区华尔街上的海关大楼，是希腊复兴

---

triangular *adj.* 三角形的   marble *n.* 大理石

downtown Manhattan, is an excellent example of Greek Revival architecture. It is a plain building, almost severe in its lack of *ornament*, but it resembles the Parthenon in Athens, Greece, in overall design. Eight Doric columns rise above a flight of steps and support a *shallow* pediment. The entire edifice is made from marble quarried just outside New York City.

建筑的杰出范例。那是一座素朴的建筑，由于不做任何装饰点缀，显得过于简朴，但总体设计却与希腊雅典帕特农神殿很相像，八根多立克式圆柱耸立于一段阶梯基座上，支撑着一道浅壁三角墙，整个大厦使用了刚出纽约城不远之处开采出来的大理石材建成。

ornament *n.* 装饰   shallow *adj.* 浅的

3

Reginald Fessenden: The Forgotten Father of Radio

The Italian physicist Guglielmo Marconi is famous as the inventor of radio. In 1895 Marconi became the first person to send *intelligible* signals from a wireless device over great distances. He later received the Nobel Prize in Physics for his work on what was then called "wireless *telegraphy*." However, it was a Canadian,

雷金纳德·费森登：被遗忘的无线电之父

意大利物理学家伽利尔摩·马可尼作为无线电的发明家闻名于世。1895年，马可尼成为实现远距离无线电可解信号传递的第一人。随后，他因自己在"无线电报"事业所做的贡献获得了诺贝尔物理学奖。然而，却是一位加拿大人——雷金纳德·费森登，发现了人嗓发出

---

intelligible *adj.* 容易理解的   telegraphy *n.* 电报

Reginald Fessenden, who discovered how to *transmit* the sound of the human voice through the air.

Fessenden's *feats* were no less remarkable than Marconi's, but his role in the development of radio is often overlooked. He seems to have had little gift for business, given that he eventually lost control of his own company. Fessenden's *patents* were vital to the development of a host of later technologies. Sadly, however, Fessenden never received the money or fame that these patents should have brought.

At the beginning of the twentieth century, most researchers in the field focused on transmitting messages through signals like the dits and dahs of Morse code. Fessenden, however, asked himself what it would take to communicate directly through speech. Wireless

---

的声音在空中是如何传递的。

　　费森登功绩的卓越并不逊于马可尼，但是他在无线电发展中的地位经常被人忽视。凭他最终落得个丧失对自己公司控制权这一地步，说明他似乎没什么经商天赋。费森登的专利对后来的许多技术研发意义重大。但遗憾的是，费森登从未获得他的专利本该带来的金钱或名誉。

　　20世纪初，这一领域的大多数研究者把精力集中于通过信号来传递信息的研究，如：摩尔斯电码"滴滴""嗒嗒"的信号传递方式。然而，费森登给自己提出的问题则是用什么办法才能直接用语言进行交际。无线

---

transmit *v.* 传导；传播　　　　　　　　　　　　　feat *n.* 功绩
patent *n.* 专利

technology had developed from discoveries about *electromagnetic* waves. Scientists knew, for instance, that energy moved through space in waves and could pass through such barriers as solid walls. Fessenden determined that waves moving at a fast but regular speed could carry sound. A receiver would convert them into sound for listeners to hear. He also determined that long, cold nights provided the best conditions for broadcasts.

On Christmas Eve in 1906, sailors aboard a fleet of ships *anchored* on the Atlantic Ocean were the first members of the public to hear human voices and the sound of a violin transmitted through wireless equipment. This program of music and readings originated in Fessenden's transmission station on the coast of Massachusetts. It

---

电科技由电磁波的发现发展而来。例如，科学家们知道能量会在波动空间中移动并且可以穿过实体墙一类的障碍物。费森登测定，快速且规律的波动可以传载声音，接收器会将波动转换成收听者可听到的声音。他还测定出，漫长而寒冷的夜晚为广播提供了最好的条件。

1906年的圣诞节前夕，在大西洋海面上抛锚停泊了一支船队，船上的海员成为了最先听到用无线电设备传递人的说话声音与小提琴乐声的听众。这个音乐和阅读节目源自费森登设于马萨诸塞州海岸的发射站，是第

---

electromagnetic *adj.* 电磁的   anchor *v.* 抛锚

was the first true radio broadcast.

Fessenden continued his experiments for the rest of his life and patented hundreds of devices. One of his most important discoveries later came to be known as sonar. In sonar, a burst of sound sent through water bounces off any object it *encounters*. By measuring the time it takes for the sound to go out and the echo to return, navigators were able to determine how far they were from the object. Fessenden's discoveries were put to immediate use by ships trying to avoid icebergs and dangerous *obstacles*. During World War I, American ships used sonic devices to locate and avoid German submarines.

一次真正的无线电广播。

　　在有生之年，费森登仍继续从事实验工作并取得了数百种装置专利权。他最重要的发明项目之一就是后来渐渐声名大噪的声纳。声纳，通过水发出的一种冲击声波，会被它遇到的物体反弹回去。通过测量声音发出去和回声返回所需的时间，领航员可以测定他们与那个物体的距离。费森登的发明立即在船只上投入使用，用来避开冰山和危险障碍物。第一次世界大战期间，美国海军利用声纳装置来定位和躲避德国潜水艇。

---

encounter *v.* 偶然遇到　　　　　　　obstacle *n.* 障碍物

4

Orson Welles and The War of the Worlds

On October 30, 1938, Orson Welles and The Mercury Theatre on the Air performed on the radio a *contemporary* adaptation of the literary classic H. G. Wells's *War of the Worlds*. The sounds of a popular dance *orchestra* were interrupted by an urgent report. It told of flames exploding from the surface of the planet

奥森·韦尔斯和《世界大战》

1938年10月30日，奥森·韦尔斯和空中水星剧场演播了一部根据赫伯特·乔治·韦尔斯的当代经典文学著作《世界大战》改编的广播剧。一段流行舞管弦乐队的音乐声被一条紧急新闻报道打断了。新闻报道叙述了火星表面发生爆炸后，烈火熊熊燃烧的场景。乐队的音乐声恢复了，但很短暂。不一会儿，一条最新报道通知听

---

contemporary *adj.* 当代的　　　　　　　　　　　orchestra *n.* 管弦乐队

Mars. The music resumed but only briefly. Soon an update informed listeners that an enormous *meteor* had fallen to Earth in New Jersey, killing thousands. As the story unfolded, audience members learned that Earth was under attack by Martian spaceships full of strange creatures armed with deadly ray guns.

The events that *transpired* next have become legend in broadcasting history. Americans panicked, jamming roads and clogging telephone lines. Some people, overcome by shock and hysteria, even went to hospitals.

Why wasn't it obvious to all listeners that the broadcast was simple entertainment? The radio schedule had been published, and the play was identified four times during the broadcast as fictitious.

众：一块巨大的陨石坠落到了地球上，就在新泽西州，造成数千人死亡。随着情节的展开，听众们了解到地球正被火星的太空船攻击，船上满载着配备致命射线枪的奇怪生物。

接下来发生的事情成了广播史上的传奇故事。美国人惊恐万分，顿时道路拥塞，电话线路无法畅通起来。有些人吓得魂飞魄散，有些人变得歇斯底里，甚至有些人去了医院接受治疗。

为什么这档显而易见的娱乐性广播节目却蒙蔽了所有的听众呢？广播时间表已经事先公布了，广播过程中也四次证实此剧纯属虚构。结果，把

---

meteor *n.* 流星　　　　　　　　　　　　　　transpire *v.* 发生

As it turns out, the number of people who were *convinced* that they were hearing about real events has been *grossly* exaggerated. Those who found the program too realistic to disbelieve were mostly older listeners. Many younger listeners were quick to recognize the narrator as Orson Welles, hero of the popular radio series *The Shadow*.

节目信以为真的人数给严重夸大了。相信的人大都是老年听众，因为节目太逼真了。许多年轻听众迅即地辨别出，剧情解说员正是著名广播系列剧《影子》的解说员——奥森·韦尔斯。

---

convince *v.* 说服　　　　　　　　　　　　　　　grossly *adv.* 严重地

5

The Makah Nation: Whale Hunters

The people of the Makah Nation have lived on Washington State's Olympic Peninsula for thousands of years. They call themselves Kwi-dich-cha-at, which means "people who live by the rocks and seagulls." The shorter name of Makah, *bestowed* on them by neighboring Native American peoples, means "generous with

马卡族：捕鲸者

马卡族人已经在华盛顿州的奥林匹克半岛上生活了数千年。他们称呼自己为"以岩石和海鸥为生的人"。马卡这个简称，是由睦邻印第安人所赠，意为"慷慨的馈食者"。

---

bestow *v.* 授予

food".

Before the arrival of the white settlers in the American Northwest, the Makah hunted gray and humpback whales from canoes made from the western red cedar tree. Whales provided meat, *blubber*, and bone for food, oil, and *utensils*. The Makah enjoyed a lively trade in whale products with other Native Americans and later with the Europeans who colonized the area. However, the Europeans' hunted the whales with an intensity and efficiency that quickly *depleted* the numbers of these creatures. The Makah relationship to the whales, on the other hand, was as much spiritual as material. Whales and whaling were subjects in their songs and dances. Images of whales were woven into blankets and baskets and carved in stone and wood. By the 1920s, with local whales on the brink of extinction, the

---

在白人拓荒者来到美国西北部之前，马卡人曾用红雪松树制成的独木舟来抓捕灰鲸和座头鲸。鲸鱼为他们提供肉类、鲸油、可食用的骨头、油和器皿。马卡人用鲸类产品与其他印第安人和后来将那片区域开拓为殖民地的欧洲人维持着频繁的贸易往来。然而，欧洲人捕杀鲸鱼的强度和效率致使这种生物的数量很快减少。另一方面，马卡人与鲸鱼的关系在精神上与物质上是同等重要的。鲸鱼和捕鲸是他们的歌曲和舞蹈的主题。鲸鱼的形象被织入毯子、篮子，也被雕刻在石头和木头上。到20世纪20年代，

---

blubber *n.* 鲸脂   utensil *n.* 器皿
deplete *v.* 耗尽；用尽

Makah stopped hunting them altogether.

Through aggressive conservation measures, whales returned to the waters off the Olympic Peninsula. In the 1970s, archeologists discovered many objects that confirmed the long and significant relationship between the Makah and whales. This awareness contributed to a cultural *resurgence* that included a focus on traditional foods and the health problems some linked to changes in the Makah diet, particularly the disappearance from it of sea mammal meat.

Eventually, the Makah decided to resume hunting whales. Although their plans faced strong opposition from different groups, they cited an 1885 treaty signed with the U.S. government that *guaranteed* them the right to continue this practice. After years of planning, the Makah

---

当地的鲸鱼濒临灭绝，马卡人才完全停止捕杀鲸鱼。

通过积极的保护措施，鲸鱼才回到奥林匹克半岛的近海水域。70年代，考古学家发现了许多文物，证实了马卡人与鲸鱼之间的长期、显著关系。这项认识有助于对马卡文化的重新关注，即关注传统食品问题以及与马卡饮食变化相关的某些健康问题，尤其是关注海洋哺乳动物肉类从马卡饮食中消失的问题。

最终，马卡人决心重新开始捕杀鲸鱼了。尽管他们的计划面对不同团体的强烈反对，他们还是援引了在1885与美国政府签署的、保障他们

---

resurgence *n.* 复苏

guarantee *v.* 确保；保证

scheduled the first hunt for the late fall of 1998. They succeeded in bringing in a gray whale about six months later. Today the Makah hunt whale in the traditional way—from large seagoing canoes, using harpoons. Divers enter the water and tie the killed whale's jaws shut to prevent the animal from sinking. The whales are finally *towed* to shore and cut into pieces in accordance with traditional *rituals*. The blubber and meat is distributed among Makah families. No part of the whale can be sold commercially, although artifacts that Makah carvers make from bones are often available for purchase.

继续捕鲸的条约。经过数年精心计划，马卡人将第一次捕鲸行动安排在了1998年深秋。6个月后，他们又成功捕获了一条灰鲸。今天，马卡人用传统方式——适于远航的大型独木舟和鱼叉来捕杀鲸鱼。潜水员潜入水中，将杀死的鲸鱼的颌骨系住以防止其下沉。再将鲸鱼拖到海岸上并依照传统习惯切割成块，并在马卡家庭中分发鲸油和肉。尽管马卡雕刻者用骨头制作的手工艺品经常可以买到，鲸鱼的任何部分都不能商业化出售。

tow *v.* 拖　　　　　　　　　　　　　　　　ritual *n.* 习俗

6

The Makah Whaling Canoe

The ancient Makah whaling canoes were *remarkable* vessels, elegant in *silhouette*, maneuverable, and seaworthy. The hull *tapered* to a point at prow and stern and rose above the center to form a graceful curve; the boat's upper edges, or *gunwales*, flared outward, a barrier that kept the interior dry despite great cresting

马卡捕鲸独木舟

古代的马卡捕鲸独木舟是不同寻常的船只，其造型美观、容易操作且适于航海。船体的船首和船尾制造成了锋利的锥形并高于船中心，形成一个优美的曲线；船舷上缘或舷缘向外倾，似一座屏障，无

---

remarkable *adj.* 不同寻常的　　　　　silhouette *n.* 轮廓
taper *v.* 逐渐变细　　　　　　　　　gunwale *n.* 船舷上缘

waves.

These enormous *cedar* dugouts were as much sculpture as construction. Their creation was governed by religious ritual and the boatmaker's knowledge. The canoes were constructed from trees that were selected and felled with care, directed downward to a safe location, and allowed to "fall gently." The tree trunk was cut to the proper length—about four-and-a-half "stretches," or the distance the boatmaker's arms can span from fingertip to fingertip. Using *implements* made of stone, bone, and shell, the boatmaker initially removed the layers of wood above the gunwales, then *flattened* the bottom, and finally hollowed out the center. When the body of the

---

论海上浪峰多巨大，都能使船体内部保持干燥。

　　这些巨大的雪松独木舟是一种建造物，同时也是一种雕塑。宗教祭仪和造船工的知识决定了巨舟能否造成。独木舟制材选用精良，所用树木都得先经人挑选，由人小心翼翼地伐倒，使其直接向下倾倒于一个安全位置，且只容许"轻轻地"倒下。将树干截成适当的长度——大约四个半"臂展"，确切地说，是造船工双臂水平展开后，从一端指尖到另一端的距离。首先，造船工利用石头、骨头和贝壳做成的工具，凿除船舷上缘的木质图层；然后，刨平船底；最后，挖出船体中心轮廓。船体加工成一定

---

cedar *n.* 雪松　　　　　　　　　　　　　　　　implement *n.* 器具
flatten *v.* 变平

canoe had been given the proper form, it was towed to the village for completion.

The interior of each canoe was painted with a mixture of fish oil and *ochre*, a mineral that produces a red color. The exterior was blackened with charcoal and oil, or sometimes lightly *scorched*, to preserve it. The elevated portions of the prow and stern were incised with decorative patterns.

形状后，要拖行到村庄里以待完工。

每条独木舟的内体结构都会刷上一种鱼油与赭石调伴的混合涂料，涂料中的赭石是一种可生成红颜色的矿物质。为了防腐，独木舟的外体结构会用木炭和油涂黑，或有时用火来轻微烧焦。船头与船尾高架的部分刻有装饰性图案。

---

ochre *n.* 赭石　　　　　　　　　　　　　　　　scorch *v.* 烧焦

7

The Fifties: Teenagers, Rebellion, and the Movies

The decade of the 1950s was a period of contrasts—of affluence and wholesome values but also of social *upheaval*. The United States seemed to be a *paradise* of comfortable houses and happy families. However, racial problems troubled much of the country. Many women discovered that they did not wish to *resume*

50年代：青少年、反叛行为和电影

20世纪50年代这十年是一段对比的时期，人们对富裕程度和有益于健康方面的价值观作对比，也对社会动荡因素作对比。美国看来是个百姓有舒适住房和幸福家庭的天堂。然而，种族问题依然困扰着这个国家的大部分地区。许多女人发现，她们并不愿意再以二战之前她们受保护的那种方式生活，对她们来说，重要的是走出家门去寻

upheaval *n.* 动乱；剧变　　　　　　　　　　paradise *n.* 天堂
resume *v.* 重新开始

the protected lives they had lived before World War II and that it was important for them to seek employment outside the home. Teenagers wondered whether a quiet life in a quiet *suburb* was what they wanted in the future. However, they represented a *potential* market for clothes, music, and entertainment, or what would one day be called popular culture.

In Hollywood, filmmakers created characters who spoke directly to this new generation, characters that were not so much heroes as antiheroes. Rather than representing the *triumph* of good over evil, they explored the tragic nature of the troubled human spirit. Two young actors—James Dean and Marlon Brando—came to personify this antihero, both in film and in real life.

Brando moved to New York City from his native Nebraska and

找工作。青少年想知道他们未来是否想在一个宁静的郊区过上一种平静的生活。可是，他们代表了一个服装、音乐和娱乐于一体的潜在市场，或者说，将来有一天它将被称作流行文化。

在好莱坞，制片人创造出了与这类新一代直接对话的人物角色，这些角色与其说是英雄不如说是反英雄。他们探索了困扰人类心灵的悲剧本质，并没有代表正义战胜邪恶。两个年轻演员——詹姆斯·迪安和马龙·白兰度在电影和真实生活中成为反英雄角色的化身。

在整个20世纪40年代，白兰度从家乡内布拉斯加州迁居纽约，并在

---

suburb *n.* 市郊；郊区   potential *adj.* 潜在的
triumph *n.* 胜利；成就

performed on Broadway throughout the 1940s. He became famous in Hollywood for his *portrayals* of angry and often unhappy young men. In 1954 Brando starred in The Wild One as the leader of a motorcycle group whose antisocial behavior in a small California community is countered by an equally unpleasant reaction from townspeople. In the film, no one seems to understand what the conflicts are about except that they are about differences between people—the young and the old, the familiar and the strange.

Dean's death in an automobile accident at the age of 24 seems to have *contributed* as much to the 1950s antihero image as the characters he portrayed in films. Dean grew up in Indiana and broke into acting while a college student in Los Angeles. In Rebel Without

---

百老汇演出。他以扮演愤怒和通常郁郁寡欢的年轻人形象闻名于好莱坞。1954年，白兰度主演影片《飞车党》中的一个飞车党头目，这个头目在加利福尼亚一个小社区的反社会行径，遭遇了市民同等程度的不愉快反应。在这部电影里，似乎无人能理解这些冲突根由何在，只知道冲突是由人与人之间的差异造成——年轻人与老年人之间的差异以及熟人与陌生人之间的差异。

24岁的迪安在一次交通事故里死于非命，这件事似乎对他成为20世纪50年代的反英雄形象和他在电影里所扮演的角色具有同样的影响。迪安

---

portrayal *n.* 扮演　　　　　　　　　　　　contribute *v.* 贡献

a Cause (1955), he portrayed a *restless*, unhappy teenager struggling to understand himself in a world that wants him to be just like everybody else.

Although these films may have *borne* little resemblance to the actual lives of teenagers, they nonetheless *struck a chord*. Many boys, and even some girls, adopted the uniform of blue jeans, T-shirt, and leather jacket worn by Brando and Dean. Films such as these, and the new music called rock-and-roll, conveyed messages of personal freedom and self-expression with which teenagers were quick to identify.

在印第安纳州长大成人，在洛杉矶读大学时闯入了演艺界。在1955年的电影《无因的反抗》中，他扮演了一个躁动不安、闷闷不乐的少年，生活在一个想要他与所有人一样的世界里，一直苦苦地挣扎求索，以真正地了解自己。

尽管这些电影可能与青少年的真实生活并不相似，但它们还是引起了青少年心中的共鸣。许多男孩，甚至一些女孩，开始接受白兰度和迪安穿的牛仔服、T恤衫和皮夹克。这类电影和称作摇滚乐的新式音乐，传达了个人自由和自我表现的信息，青少年很快与这些信息产生了强烈共鸣。

restless *adj.* 焦躁不安的　　　　　　　bear *v.* 带有（某种标记或特征）
strike a chord 引起共鸣

8

Movie Fad of the Fifties: Seeing in 3-D

Many people felt a *twinge* of *nostalgia* when Sidney Pink died in 2002. Pink, an actor and producer, was known as the "father of the feature-length three-dimensional (3-D) movie," a popular 1950s art form.

Shooting film in 3-D required the operator to *synchronize* the timing of cameras

---

50年代的电影时尚：3–D 电影

2002年悉尼·平克去世时，许多人心中泛起了一阵阵怀旧之情。作为演员和制片人，平克以 "正片时长的三维（3D）电影之父"著称于世，这类电影是50年代一种流行的艺术形式。

拍摄3D电影，要求摄像师使放得很近的（两部）摄像机同步开机拍

---

twinge *n.* 一阵强烈情感　　　　　　　　　　nostalgia *n.* 怀旧
synchronize *v.* 使同步

set inches apart. In the theater, the images produced by two projectors were *aligned* on a single screen. Audience members wore special colored glasses that emphasized minor differences between the images; one viewer described the experience as having the action jump off the screen and into her lap. Watching a 3-D film could be alarming, and people were known to faint, duck, or flee from the theater.

The startling effects of 3-D technology were particularly well suited to horror movies. The first 3-D film, *Bwana Devil*, which Pink coproduced, is the story of two hungry lions that *terrorize* an area in Africa. In *Creature from the Black Lagoon*, a group of scientists travel to South America to locate a strange monster that is half human and

---

摄。在电影院里，两台放映机产生的影像要在一个单独的屏幕上校准。观众们佩戴可分辨映像间微小差别的特制有色眼镜；一位观众这样描绘她的体验——就像情节跳出屏幕到了她身上。看3D电影会使人恐慌不已，人们会昏晕、躲避或逃出电影院。

3D技术的惊人效果特别适用于恐怖电影。第一部平克与人合作拍摄的3D电影《非洲历险记》，讲述了两只饥饿的狮子使非洲一个地区人们生活在恐惧中的故事。在《黑湖怪兽》中，一群科学家赴南美去寻找一只

---

align *v.* 与……结盟　　　　　　　　　　　　　　terrorize *v.* 恐吓

half fish. *Creature from the Black* Lagoon became a *cult* favorite; *sequels* to the original include *Revenge of the Creature* and *The Creature Walks Among Us*. The novelty of 3-D movies quickly faded, however, and filmmakers had generally abandoned the technology by the decade's end.

半人半鱼的怪兽。《黑湖怪兽》受到了人们的狂热喜爱，原著的续集包括《怪物的复仇》和《走在我们之间的怪物》。然而，3D电影的新颖性快速消退了，在50年代快要结束之际，制片人们通常已经放弃这项技术了。

---

cult *adj.* 受到猛烈崇拜的   sequel *n.* 续篇；续集

9

Tycoons and Antitrust Laws

One thinks of princes and presidents as some of the most powerful people in the world; however, governments, elected or otherwise, sometimes have had to struggle with the financial *powerhouses* called tycoons. The word tycoon is *relatively* new to the English language. It is Chinese in origin but was given as a title to some

企业大亨和反垄断法

有人认为王子和总统是世界上最有权力的人；然而，选举产生的政府或其他方式产生的政府，有时要与称作大亨的金融权贵展开较量。"大亨"一词是英语中较近时期出现的新词语。它源于中文，旧时用来指称日本将军。19世纪末，这一专用语传到美国，最终用来指称

---

powerhouse *n.* 权威人士；权势集团   relatively *adv.* 相对地

Japanese generals. The term was brought to the United States, in the late nineteenth century, where it eventually was used to refer to *magnates* who acquired immense fortunes from sugar and cattle, coal and oil, rubber and steel, and railroads. Some people called these tycoons "captains of industry" and praised them for their contributions to U.S. wealth and international stature. Others criticized them as ruthless "robber barons," who would stop at nothing in pursuit of personal wealth.

The early tycoons built successful businesses, often taking over smaller companies to eliminate competition. A single company that came to control an entire market was called a *monopoly*. Monopolies made a few families very wealthy, but they also placed a heavy financial burden on consumers and the economy at large.

靠制糖、畜牧、煤碳、石油、橡胶、钢铁以及铁路等产业获取巨额财富的大企业家。有些人将这些大亨称为"工业巨头"，赞誉他们在为美国积累财富和创造国际水平中所做出的贡献。另外一些人则批评他们为冷酷无情的、永不停止追求个人财富的"强盗大亨"。

　　早期的企业大亨们经常通过收购更小的公司来消除竞争，从而成功创业。单独的一家公司控制了整个市场叫做垄断。垄断使一些家族非常富有，但是他们整体上也给消费者和经济增加了沉重的财政负担。

---

magnate *n.* 巨头；大亨　　　　　　　　　　　　monopoly *n.* 垄断

As the country expanded and railroads linked the East Coast to the West Coast, local monopolies turned into national corporations called trusts. A trust is a group of companies that join together under the control of a board of *trustees*. Railroad trusts are an excellent example. Railroads were privately owned and operated and often monopolized various routes, setting rates as high as they desired. The financial burden this placed on passengers and businesses increased when railroads formed trusts. Farmers, for example, had no choice but to pay, as railroads were the only means they could use to get their grain to buyers. *Exorbitant* freight rates put some farmers out of business.

There were even *accusations* that the trusts controlled government itself by buying votes and *manipulating* elected officials. In 1890

随着国家版图的扩张和连接东西海岸铁路的修建，地方垄断转变成了叫做托拉斯的全国性公司。托拉斯是一个在董事会控制下的、由一些公司联合起来组成的机构。以铁路托拉斯为典例，铁路为私人拥有和经营，各种铁路专线受到长期垄断，运输费被定到最高值。当铁路形成托拉斯时，它们加于旅客和企业的财政负担就会增大。就拿农场主来说，面临运费涨价时，他们别无选择只能付费，因为铁路是农场主所能利用把粮食运送给买方的唯一途径。过于高昂的运费致使一些农场主破产。

甚至有人指控托拉斯通过购买选票和操纵当选的官员来控制政府。

---

trustee *n.* 受托人
accusation *n.* 指责；指控

exorbitant *adj.* 过高的
manipulate *v.* 控制；操纵

Congress passed the Sherman Antitrust Act, legislation aimed at breaking the power of such trusts. The Sherman Antitrust Act focused on two main issues. First of all, it made illegal any effort to interfere with the normal conduct of *interstate* trade. It also made it illegal to monopolize any part of business that operates across state lines.

Over the next 60 years or so, Congress enacted other antitrust laws in an effort to encourage competition and *restrict* the power of large corporations.

1890年，国会通过了《谢尔曼反托拉斯法》，目的在于破坏这种托拉斯权力。《谢尔曼反托拉斯法》主要强调了两个问题：首先，凡干预州际贸易正常进行的做法属于违法。其次，凡跨越州界对某部分产业进行垄断经营的行为亦属违法。

在随后60年左右的时间里，国会又颁布了一些反垄断法令，以激励竞争和限制大型公司的权力。

---

interstate *adj.* 州际的   restrict *v.* 限制

10

Henry Clay Frick: A Mixed Legacy

A visit to the Frick Collection in New York City inspires admiration for the man who created the museum as a gift for future generations. The mansion built by Henry Clay Frick houses a treasury of paintings, *bronze* sculptures, Chinese *porcelain*, and exquisite furniture. His *philanthropy* went beyond the visual arts. His

亨利·克莱·弗里克：毁誉参半的遗产

去纽约市弗里克美术博物馆参观，人们会对亨利·克莱·弗里克产生出一种钦佩之情，原因是他创立了这座博物馆，并将它作为厚礼传给后世。弗里克创建的这座大厦又有宝馆之称，馆内收藏了油画、青铜雕塑、中国瓷器和精美家俱。他的捐款还资助了许多科学和公共

---

bronze *n.* 青铜   porcelain *n.* 瓷
philanthropy *n.* 慈善；博爱

contributions also supported projects related to the sciences and public education. In his will, he left about $36 million to organizations that aided the public. Yet to describe Frick only as kindly or *benevolent* would paint a *misleading* picture.

A self-made millionaire by the age of 30, Frick quickly learned how to turn the misfortunes of others to his own gain. His company mined coal and then refined it into *coke* that it sold to steel factories. He eventually joined Andrew Carnegie's steel business, helping to create a monopoly on mining, steel, and railroad operations. This tycoon known as a ruthless businessman locked striking workers out of the Homestead steel mill during contract talks and brought in 300

教育工程，不难料定，他所秉持的这种慈善精神已超越了视觉艺术。在遗嘱里，他遗留给公益组织的善款总计约3 600万美元。但是，把弗里克只描述为仁厚或慈善之君会是一种误导。

从白手起家到30岁成为百万富翁，弗里克很快就知道了怎样将别人的厄运转换为自己的财运。他的公司先开采原煤，其后将原煤精炼为焦炭，再将焦炭出售给钢铁厂。最终，他加盟了安德鲁·卡耐基的钢铁产业，并在把煤矿、钢铁和铁路创建为一个垄断实体过程中立下了汗马之

---

benevolent *adj.* 仁慈的　　　　　　　　　　　**misleading** *adj.* 误导性的
coke *n.* 焦炭

armed detectives who fired on, and killed, several of the *protestors*. Frick ordered the strikers' families *evicted* from company-owned houses and made it impossible for many strikers to find another job in the business. After the strike ended, Frick was attacked in his office but survived. He died in 1919.

功。这位素以"无情商人"著称的企业大亨在谈判还在进展之时将罢工工人锁在荷姆斯泰德钢铁厂大门外，并请来了300名武装警探，对工人们开火，使数名抗议者遇难。弗里克命令将罢工者的家属从工厂职工宿舍中驱逐出去，并且使许多罢工者无法在钢铁行业再找到另一份工作。罢工结束后，弗里克在他的办公室遭受袭击，但幸存了下来。他于1919年辞世。

protestor *n.* 抗议者 　　　　　　　　　　　　　　　　 evict *v.* 驱逐

11

The Protestant Reformation:Changes in Religion, Changes in Society

The Protestant Reformation began in 1516 when Martin Luther challenged certain practices in the Roman Catholic Church. Luther was a Catholic *priest* whose study of the Bible led him to reject many of the Church's teachings. He was not the first person to *cast* doubt on these teachings, or on the authority of the Pope in Rome. His

新教改革：改变宗教，改变社会

新教改革开始于1516年，当时马丁·路德对罗马天主教的某些习惯提出了质疑。路德是一位因为研究圣经而导致自己拒绝接受许多教会教义的天主教牧师。他并不是对这些教义或罗马教皇的权力提出

---

priest *n.* 牧师；神父

cast *v.* 使人生疑

challenge, however, signaled the end of the Church's *dominance* in European culture.

The reform movement—with its notion that salvation was solely a matter of faith—attracted much popular support. Reformers criticized the practice of selling *indulgences* as a means by which people could "pay" their way into Heaven. When the Bible was translated from Latin into English, French, and German, people began to read the Scriptures themselves instead of relying on interpretations offered by the *clergy*. In fact, some reformers said that priests, along with their ritual practices and prayers, were no longer needed.

The desire to change what many regarded as corrupt practices

质疑的第一人。然而，他的质疑标志着教会对欧洲文化统治的结束。

改革运动观念——将救赎作为唯一信仰要素，吸引了多数民众的支持。改革者批评将出售赎罪券的做法看成是人们支付天堂路费的一种方式。当圣经从拉丁文译成英文、法文和德文时，人们开始自己阅读经文，而不再依靠神职人员的翻译。实际上，有些改革者说牧师连同牧师们的仪式与祷告，已经不再为人所需。

然而，期望改变教会里的腐败行径并不是改革背后的唯一动力。在欧

---

dominance *n.* 统治地位　　　　　　　　　　　　indulgence *n.* 纵容

clergy *n.* 教士

in the Church was not the only *impetus* behind the Reformation, however. In Europe this period was one of widespread political *turmoil*. From the Church's point of view, its realm encompassed all of humanity and observed no national borders. The nobility, however, disagreed. They envied the Church for its landholdings and resented the taxes that the *aristocrats* and their subjects had to pay the Church. The nobles disliked in particular the Church's involvement in secular matters such as the law and business. Some regions wanted to end rule by the Holy Roman Empire (HRE), which controlled most of Eastern Europe and Germany. The HRE and the Church were traditional allies; action taken against one implied resistance to the other.

A number of developments gave *momentum* to the Reformation.

洲，这段时期恰是政治混乱的扩散期之一。从教会的角度看，这种扩散不分国界，囊括了全人类社会。然而，贵族持反对态度。他们嫉妒教会拥有土地，且因他们和属民必须向教会纳税而怨恨不已。贵族尤其憎恨教会对法律和商业等世俗问题的介入。有些地区想要结束神圣罗马帝国对东欧和德国大部分地区的统治。神圣罗马帝国和教会是传统的联盟，对其中一个采取反对行动也意味着反抗另一个。

多数技术发展为改革提供了动力。15世纪50年代，印刷机的发明使

---

impetus *n.* 推动力；促进因素　　　　turmoil *n.* 混乱；骚动
aristocrat *n.* 贵族　　　　momentum *n.* 势头

The invention of the printing press in the 1450s made books less costly. This led to a rise in *literacy* rates. A middle class made up of merchants, craftspeople, and manufacturers emerged. New industries, technologies, and global trade created opportunities and wealth.

Improvements in the economy and education—and a greater sense of nationalism—also played a part. Members of the nobility, particularly in Germany, embraced the new ideas and used them to challenge the power of both the pope and the emperor. In countries throughout Europe, church and state *wrestled* to find a balance, in a struggle that in many ways continues to this day.

书籍成本大幅降低，从而提高了识字率。由商人、手工艺人和生产商组成的中产阶级出现了。新兴工业、科技和全球贸易创造了机遇与财富。

经济和教育状况的改善以及更加强烈的民族感也发挥了一份作用。贵族成员，尤其是德国的贵族成员，接受了新思想并运用新思想去挑战教皇和君主的权力。在欧洲各国，教会和国家相互争斗与较量以寻求平衡，许多方面的斗争直到今天还在持续。

---

literacy *n.* 读写能力   wrestle *v.* 试图解决

12

The Modern Amish: Descendents of the Anabaptists

Horse-drawn *buggies* are a familiar sight in Lancaster County, Pennsylvania. So are bearded men in black hats and women in plain dresses covered by *aprons* with their hair tucked up under caps. These people are the Amish. Their ancestors immigrated to America in search of religious freedom during the early

现代阿米什人：再洗礼派的后裔

宾夕法尼亚州兰卡斯特郡的常景之一当属它的四轮单马轻便马车了。另一常景就是：郡上的男人戴黑色礼帽、蓄着胡须；女人衣着朴素、裙子上覆盖着围裙并将头发折卷在帽子下面。这些人就是阿米什人。18世纪初，他们的祖先为寻求宗教自由移民到了美洲。除英语外，

---

buggy n. 轻便小马车   apron n. 围裙

eighteenth century. They speak a *dialect* of German, in addition to English, and are sometimes referred to as the "Pennsylvania Dutch" because the word for "German"—deutsch—was misunderstood to mean "Dutch."

The Amish are descendents of the Anabaptists, a *sect* that rejected infant *baptism*. It emerged at the time of the Protestant Reformation. A leader of the Anabaptists was Jacob Amman, who lived in Switzerland in the early sixteenth century. Amman and his followers opposed any kind of state church. They were pacifists, so many refused to fight in wars. Some believed it immoral to vote or take part in government. The modern Amish continue to organize their

---

他们还讲一种德国方言。有时他们会被称作"宾夕法尼亚荷兰人"，因为用以形容"德国人"的单词——"deutsch"被误解成了"Dutch"。

阿米什人是再洗礼派的后裔，这个宗派不接受婴儿洗礼。它是在新教改革运动时出现的。再洗礼派的领导者之一是16世纪初住在瑞士的雅各·阿曼。阿曼和他的追随者反对任何形式的国家教会。他们是和平主义者，所以许多人拒绝参战。有些人认为投票或加入政府是不道德的。现代阿米什人继续围绕其虔诚精神性来安排他们的生活，并将自己与尘世杂念

---

dialect *n.* 方言

baptism *n.* 洗礼

sect *n.* 宗派；派别

lives around spirituality and to separate themselves from worldly concerns such as politics and modern technology.

Today Amish communities exist throughout the United States and Canada. The Old Order Amish, most traditional of all, *worship* in their homes. They generally *eschew* automobiles, electricity, telephones, and high school education. Living in conscious simplicity, they focus on their families and their faith.

隔离，比如，政治和现代科技。

现在，阿米什社区遍布美国和加拿大。旧时安曼教派，是所有阿米什人最为传统的一支，安曼教徒都在家中做礼拜。通常，他们避讳用汽车、电力、电话以及让子女接受中学教育。他们注重个人家庭和信仰，并着意于过淳朴的生活。

worship *v.* 敬奉（神）；崇拜   eschew *v.* 躲开；躲避

13

Pharoah Akhenaten and the Amarna Period

Pharoah Akhenaten's 17-year reign in Egypt was significant for several reasons. He married the *legendary* Nefertiti, with whom he had six daughters. He also replaced the *pantheon* of Egyptian deities with a single god named Aten and built a new capital, Akhetaten, in the north at a location that is now known as Tell el-

法老阿克那顿和阿玛纳时期

埃及法老阿克那顿在位17年的政绩之所以显赫主要有如下原因：他娶了传奇女子奈费尔提蒂并与她孕育了六个女儿；他还用名为阿托恩的一位神取代了供奉埃及神明的万神殿，并在如今叫做特勒埃尔阿玛纳的一个地方的北部建立了一座新都会——阿克塔顿。阿克那顿的统

---

legendary *adj.* 传奇般的　　　　　　　　　　pantheon *n.* 众神；诸神

Amarna. Akhenaten's reign is often called the Amarna period.

The god Aten was *envisioned* as the light within the sun's disk; he was the source of life and all that was *virtuous*, and the creator of human beings. The fundamental principle of Aten worship was that of ma'at, or *divine* truth. The idea of ma'at was also expressed in a goddess (Ma'at), who represented the principles of order, balance, and justice.

Aten worship was very ancient. This cult had attracted members for more than 1,000 years. Raising Aten worship to the level of official religion, however, may have been part of Akhenaten's plan to tighten his control over the government. His father, Amenhotep III, had been troubled by the growing political power of the priests.

治经常被称为阿玛纳时期。

　　人们将阿托恩神想象为日轮神之光，它是生命和道德之源，也是人类的创造者。阿托恩崇拜的根本原则即：崇拜真理和正义，这些原则由象征秩序、平衡和正义的女神玛特向人们表达。

　　阿托恩崇拜源远流长，这种崇拜吸引着信徒足足一千多年。然而，将阿托恩崇拜提升到正式宗教的水平也许是阿克那顿加强他对政府控制的计划的一部分。他的父亲阿蒙霍泰普三世就受到祭司不断增长的政治势力所困扰。阿克那顿试着通过降低祭司们所信奉之神的重要性来削弱他们的势

---

envision *v.* 设想；想象　　　　　　　virtuous *adj.* 有德行的；道德高尚的
divine *adj.* 神圣的

Akhenaten tried to weaken the priests by reducing the importance of the gods they served. The old capital of Thebes, in southern Egypt, remained a *stronghold* of the old priests; but the new capital, Akhetaten, which means "horizon of the Aten," was built on ground that had few if any connections to gods.

Akhenaten encouraged his artists to develop a new style, one that stressed what was human and natural rather than what was *awe* inspiring and godlike. Temples to Aten were not enclosed, mysterious interiors. They were open courtyards filled with sunlight. In painting and sculpture, informal images of the pharaoh and his family replaced formal, idealized *portraits*. One well-known limestone relief shows Akhenaten and his queen, Nefertiti, seated face to face.

力。位于埃及南部的旧都会底比斯，依然是旧祭司们的大本营；但是新都会，意为"阿托恩地平线"的阿克塔顿，被修建在与神几乎没有关系的地方。

阿克那顿鼓励艺术家们发展一种新的艺术形式，强调一切人性化和自然的事物，而不强调一切让人心感敬畏和神一般的事物。阿托恩神殿并不是封闭而神秘的内室，而是洒满阳光的开阔庭院。在绘画和雕刻上，法老和他家人不拘礼节的形象取代了正规和理想化的肖像。一幅著名石灰岩浮雕展现了阿克那顿和他的皇后奈费尔提蒂对面而坐的情景。阿克那顿亲吻

---

stronghold *n.* （持共同态度或信仰的人的）大本营   awe *n.* 敬畏
portrait *n.* 肖像

Akhenaten kisses one of his daughters while his wife embraces two others. Between them the disk of Aten sends down its blessings in the form of rays. Akhenaten himself looks *ungainly*, with a thin *torso* and wide hips. Scholars continue to argue today about whether these images are realistic or simply show a different standard of beauty.

Akhenaten's new religion did not survive his *reign*. He had been a weak ruler and had offended many powerful people. It seems unlikely, too, that most common people had accepted Aten worship. Akhenaten's successors quickly allied themselves with the priests, who were determined to restore the other Egyptian gods.

着一个女儿，他的妻子怀抱着另外两个。阿托恩神在他们之间降下了祝福之光。阿克那顿其貌不扬，有一副瘦瘦的躯干和肥阔的臀部。关于这些形象是否属实或描述者只是为了展示美的不同标准，学者们至今仍然争论不休。

阿克那顿推行的新宗教并没有使他的统治得以幸存。他是个软弱的统治者，并冒犯了许多有权势的人。看起来，也不像是有大部分平民接受了阿托恩崇拜。阿克那顿的继任者很快与决心复位其他埃及神明的祭司们结成了同盟。

---

ungainly *adj.* 难看的   torso *n.* （人体的）躯干
reign *n.* 统治；治理

14

The Amarna Tablets

Tell el Amarna—meaning "the hill Amarna"—is the modern name for the ancient ruins located *alongside* the Nile River in central Egypt. This place was once an important city, rich with palaces and temples, and the center of worship for the cult of Aten.

In 1887 a woman digging in the area

阿玛尔那泥板

特勒埃尔阿玛尔那，意为阿玛尔那山，是座落于埃及中部尼罗河畔古代遗址的现称。这个地方曾经是一个很重要的城市，有许多的宫殿和寺院，也是阿托恩神拜觐中心。

1887年，一位在这块区域里铲土的妇女收集了一堆泥板，并把它们

---

alongside *prep.* 在……旁边

collected a pile of clay tablets and carried them home. It was not long before *antiquities* dealers, archeologists, and historians *converged* on the site, attracted by rumors of a valuable hoard. Eventually, about 380 tablets, whole and fragmentary, were unearthed.

The tablets date from the middle of the fourteenth century B.C. The majority of them are letters sent to pharaohs Amenhotep III and his son Akhenaten from countries that were part of the vast Egyptian empire, including Babylonia and Assyria.

The tablets are made of clay—some of them extremely small, less than three inches square. The letters are cuneiform, a system of writing developed in the region of Mesopotamia. The characters

---

带回了家。不久，那里出了座宝库的消息不胫而走，古董商、考古学家和历史学家们被传闻所吸引，一起汇聚到了出宝之地。最终，大约有380块完整或残缺的泥板出土。

泥版的历史可追溯到公元前14世纪中叶。泥板大多数为书信，从辽阔埃及帝国的部分城邦，巴比伦和亚述等地发出，寄给法老阿蒙霍泰普三世和他的儿子阿克那顿。

这些泥板是用黏土做成的，其中一些特别小，还不到三平方英寸。撰写那些信采用了楔形文字，即一种在美索不达米亚地区发展而来的文字系

---

antiquity *n.* 古物；古迹   converge *v.* 汇集；聚集

were pressed into the *damp* clay with a wedge-shaped stylus, or stick, and then the clay was baked in an oven or dried to harden it. A young German schoolteacher first *deciphered* cuneiform writing in the early 1800s, and what was written thousands of years ago now can be understood.

统。用楔形铁笔或木棍将文字压入潮湿的黏土中，然后，将黏土置于烤炉中烘烤使之变硬。19世纪初，一位年轻的德国教师最先译解了楔形文字，现在人们可以理解写于几千年前的文字了。

---

damp *adj.* 潮湿的；微湿的   decipher *v.* 破译；译解

15

Corn in the Legends of the Sioux

The Sioux people, who once lived throughout the Great Plains from Iowa to Montana, are famous for the *triangular*, portable homes, called tepees, in which they lived, and for their talents as horse riders and buffalo hunters. Less familiar, perhaps, is their literature. These stories were *altered* in each retelling as

苏族传说中的玉米

苏族人，曾居住于从爱荷华州到蒙大拿州的大平原地区，以居住可移动圆锥形帐篷和骑马与猎捕野牛的本领闻名于世。也许他们的文学不太为人所熟知，原因在于家长给孩子讲故事时，每一次都有所改动。他们讲述的故事主要涉及苏族人的生存环境、鸟类、动物、地理与

---

triangular *adj.* 三角（形）的   alter *v.* 改变；更改

they were passed down from parents to children. The stories dealt with the Sioux's environment and its birds and animals, geography, and weather. Recurring characters included Unktomi, a *mischievous* spider whose appearance generally foretold misfortune. Corn, a basic part of the Sioux diet for more than 1,000 years, was another popular subject for legends.

According to tradition, corn was introduced in the Sioux world by way of a hermit, a medicine man who lived a *solitary* existence in the forest distant from Sioux villages. Irritated by nightly visitations from some mysterious being, the hermit finally shot an arrow into the dark. The next morning, he discovered *kernels* scattered on the ground outside, and when he dug down into the earth at the trail's end, he

---

气候。故事中有一个反复出现的、名为恩科托米的角色———一只顽皮的蜘蛛，它的出现通常预示着不幸。玉米，作为苏族饮食的一个基本成分已经有一千多年的历史，是传说的另一个极受人们喜爱的主题。

据故事传说，将玉米引进苏人世界中的是一位隐士。他是一个巫医，一个人在远离苏族村落的森林里过着独居生活。由于隐士夜夜都受到某神秘生物降临的烦扰，他最终朝黑暗处射了一支箭。第二天清晨，他发现外面的地上洒满了玉米粒，而且当他在小路尽头挖掘土坑时，他发现了里面

---

mischievous *adj.* 调皮的；淘气的   solitary *adj.* 独处的；独居的
kernel *n.* 仁；核

discovered leather sacks filled with dried meat and cherries—and the precious corn.

Corn was so valuable to the Sioux that not a kernel was to be wasted. Legend told of a woman who, having harvested the corn, was leaving the cornfield when an *anguished* and persistent voice pleaded for her attention. The woman searched *diligently* for the speaker and eventually located one tiny ear of corn that was hidden underneath some leaves. Another Sioux legend held that the appearance of the corn reflected the character of the person who planted it. Cornstalks growing in straight lines and producing large ears full of kernels were evidence that an individual was truthful and *conscientious*. An ear containing a few kernels separated by empty

---

装满肉干和樱桃的皮革袋——还有珍贵的玉米。

玉米对苏族人来说极其珍贵，哪怕一个玉米粒也不会浪费。有这样一则传说：曾有一位妇女，当她收获玉米要离开玉米地时，一个极其痛苦的、持续的声音央求她注意。这名妇女努力顺着声音方向找去，最终找到了埋藏在一些玉米叶子下面的一小穗玉米。另一则传说认为，玉米的品相反映了玉米播种人的性格。垂直挺拔的玉米秆和结出丰满颗粒的硕大玉米穗表明一个人做事诚实和认真的品格。一穗间隙大、颗粒稀疏的玉米往往表示这个人会活到很老，老到她的牙会变得少且稀疏。最后，一根玉米秆

---

anguished *adj.* 痛苦不堪的　　　　　diligently *adv.* 勤奋地；细致彻底地
conscientious *adj.* 认真的

spaces was an indication that the individual would live to be so old that her teeth would be few and far between. Finally, a cornstalk on which many small ears *sprouted* from the base of a large one symbolized a large and respectable family.

Among the Sioux people, corn agriculture was the responsibility of the women, from the sorting and *germination* of the seed to the preparation of the ground. After transplanting four sprouts into each mound of dirt, they offered prayers to the Great Spirit for blessings on their work and for the balance of summer sunshine and rain needed for a plentiful harvest.

上面结一大穗玉米，在其底部发出许多小穗玉米，往往象征这是一个人丁兴旺、受人尊敬的家庭。

在苏族人当中，一切玉米农活皆由女人们承担，从选种、发芽到土地备耕。当把四株幼苗移栽到每一个小土堆里之后，她们会祈求大神降福于她们的辛苦劳作，赐予她们风调雨顺的年景，以获得一年的大丰收。

---

sprout *v.* 发芽；生长　　　　　　　germination *n.* 发芽

16

Alice Cunningham Fletcher

Alice Cunningham Fletcher was an unusual woman for her time. Born in 1838, she taught school and worked tirelessly to *advance* women's rights. Her interest in history led her to study *archeology* at the Peabody Museum at Harvard University. When she was in her forties, she traveled to the Dakota Territory to observe

艾利斯·坎宁安·弗莱彻

艾利斯·坎宁安·弗莱彻，出生于1838年；从事教书职业，一直为提高女性权益而不知疲倦地工作；是她那个时代的一名非凡女性。对历史的兴趣促使她前往哈佛大学皮博迪博物馆学习考古学。四十多岁时，她赴达科他地区旅行，观察苏族妇女日常生活。她写了满满两日

---

advance *v.* 推动；促进　　　　　　　　archeology *n.* 考古学

the daily life of Sioux women. She filled two journals with records of her experiences and made more than 60 drawings. Her notes include the texts of stories translated for her by her assistant, an Omaha Sioux named Susette La Flesche.

Fletcher's interest in Native Americans grew to concern about the poverty in which most of them lived. The U.S. Congress *consulted* with her, and she worked briefly for the Bureau of Indian Affairs. She also *lobbied* for the protection of Native American ruins.

Although Fletcher's efforts were both *altruistic* and sincere, she shared the common belief that all cultures should be judged by the progress they had made from "savagery" toward "civilization."

记本的见闻，还足足画了60多幅简图。她的见闻录中包含一些故事文本。这些文本均是一位名叫苏泽特·拉弗莱彻（她的奥马哈苏族人助手）的人协助她翻译成文。

随着弗莱彻对印第安人的兴趣愈加浓厚，她更加关注起大部分印第安人的贫困生活。美国国会向她咨询印第安人的生活情况。她曾在印第安人事务局短期工作过一段时间。再者，她还为保护印第安人遗址游说过议员。

尽管弗莱彻的努力无私而真诚，但她也赞同一种普遍的信念，即所有

---

consult *v.* 咨询；请教　　　　　　lobby *v.* 向……进行游说
altruistic *adj.* 利他的；无私的

She thought that Native Americans should become more like white Americans in order to achieve economic and social success.

By the time of her death in 1923, Fletcher was widely respected for her many books and articles about Native American stories, songs, games, dances, *costumes*, and religious *ceremonies*.

文化都该用从"野蛮"到"文明"的进步来评判。她认为印第安人要获得经济和社会的成功应该变得更像美国白人。

到1923年她去世之前，弗莱彻因为她编辑和撰写许多关于美国印第安人故事、歌曲、游戏、舞蹈、服装和宗教仪式等方面的书籍和文章而广受尊敬。

---

costume *n.* 戏服；服装　　　　　　　　　ceremony *n.* 仪式；典礼

17

Taos, New Mexico: An Artists' Colony

By the middle of the nineteenth century in the United States, stories of the *scenic* beauties of the northern New Mexico Territory had already caught the attention of people living back East. Then, in 1898, a couple of young artists on a painting *expedition* in the West found themselves stranded in Taos after a wagon

新墨西哥的陶斯小镇：艺术家的领地

截至19世纪中叶，有关新墨西哥领地北部地区风光纷外绮丽的传闻已经引起了美国东部人的关注。1898年，一场车祸发生后，几位在西部做绘画考察的年轻艺术家被困在了陶斯小镇。他们陶醉于小镇的自然风景和光线，于是，他们召集了一些朋友并与他们共同创立了陶斯

scenic *adj.* 景色优美的   expedition *n.* 远足；探险

accident. *Enchanted* by the landscape and the light, they, along with a few friends, founded the Taos Society of Artists. By the 1920s, artists, writers, and others had turned a rural village into a sophisticated art colony. By the 1930s and 1940s, the colony's *allure* was international.

The home of writer and socialite Mabel Dodge Luhan became for many the center of the Taos community. Born to a wealthy family from Buffalo, New York, she was famous as a generous, if *eccentric*, hostess. Her homes in Florence, Italy, and New York City were a magnet for artists, journalists, actors, and activists. She dedicated herself to causes she thought would make American society more open and modern. An *ardent* pacifist, she had published many articles protesting the U.S. entry into World War I.

艺术家协会。到20世纪20年代，艺术家、作家和其他艺术界同仁已经将一个农村小镇转变成了一个高级艺术领地。到20世纪30年代和20世纪40年代，这块艺术领地又透射出了国际化的魅力。

梅布尔·道奇·卢汉，既为作家同时又是社交名流，对许多人来说，她的家成了陶斯艺术社区的中心。她出生于纽约水牛城的一个富裕家庭，虽脾气时有古怪，却以乐善好施而闻名。她在意大利佛罗伦萨和纽约市的家如磁石一般吸引着众多艺术家、记者、演员和活动家光顾。她致力于那些她认为可以让美国社会更为开放和更加现代化的事业。作为一名热忱的和平主义者，她发表了许多抗议美国参加第一次世界大战的文章。

---

enchant *v.* 使陶醉；使入迷

eccentric *adj.* 古怪的；怪异的

allure *n.* 诱惑力；魅力

ardent *adj.* 热心的

Mabel Dodge moved to Taos in 1918, convinced that she had found a sort of paradise, a place of *innocence* and purity. Its Native American culture, from her point of view, was peaceful and spiritual, unlike the stressful and violent lives led by the "Anglos." She eventually married a Taos Pueblo Indian named Tony Luhan and gathered about her the most creative and interesting people of the time. Writers such as Willa Cather and D. H. Lawrence and painters such as Georgia O'Keeffe came to stay in the complex of buildings that belonged to the "big house". Many of Luhan's guests, including Lawrence and O'Keeffe, later bought houses of their own nearby. Luhan died in 1962, but the world she helped create remains very much alive.

Today the *rugged* but lovely landscape of the Sangre de Cristo

---

1918年，梅布尔·道奇搬到了陶斯，她深信自己发现了一个天堂，一块天真和纯洁之地。依她所看，那里的印第安人文化安宁而圣洁，与此迥然不同，"盎格鲁人"过着充满压力和野蛮暴力的生活。她最终嫁给了一位名为托尼·卢汉的陶斯布洛印第安人，并将那个时代最有创造力和情趣的人都聚集到了她的身边。比方说，作家威拉·卡瑟和劳伦斯以及画家乔治亚·欧姬芙都曾光顾和客居于她家的"大房子"建筑群之内。后来，卢汉的许多客人，包括劳伦斯和欧姬芙在内，都在附近自己买了房子。卢汉逝世于1962年，但由她倾力创建的世界依然保持着蓬勃生机。

如今，桑格里克利托斯山崎岖而美丽的风景还在吸引着艺术家和作

---

innocence n. 天真；单纯

rugged adj. 崎岖的

Mountains continues to attract artists and writers. The Taos Pueblo, an ancient group of *adobe* structures rising several stories in height, is believed to have been occupied for at least 800 years. Also in Taos is the San Francisco de Assisi Mission Church, built in the eighteenth century. Its simple *sculptural* form is a popular theme for painters and photographers. Taos provides creative inspiration in *myriad* ways, from writing workshops and art schools to film festivals and Native American powwows.

家。陶斯部落建筑群，一组几层楼高的古老土坯结构建筑，据说有人居住的历史至少已有800年了。在陶斯，还有一座建于18世纪的圣芳济亚西西大教堂，它简约的雕刻形式是画家和摄影师的一个热门主题。陶斯以多种方式为人们提供了创作灵感，从写作研讨会、艺术学校到电影节和印第安人仪式等应有尽有。

adobe *n.* 土坯   sculptural *adj.* 雕刻的

myriad *adj.* 无数的；各种各样的

18

Georgia O'Keeffe

The artist Georgia O'Keeffe was born in Wisconsin, was *brought up* in Virginia, and lived much of her adult life in New York City. The place she loved most, however, was New Mexico.

O'Keeffe had first visited New Mexico in 1917 while on vacation with her sister. In 1929 she returned at the invitation of writer

乔治亚·欧姬芙

艺术家乔治亚·欧姬芙出生于威斯康辛州，在弗吉尼亚州长大成人，成年后，她的大多数时光在纽约市度过。然而，她最爱的地方是新墨西哥。

1917年，欧姬芙与她姐姐一起度假时，第一次游览了新墨西哥州。

---

bring up 养育；抚养

Mabel Dodge Luhan. The landscape, the light, and most of all the *solitude* suited O'Keeffe's rather *taciturn* temperament perfectly. The paintings for which she was already famous were simple, almost abstract, portrayals of skyscrapers and flowers, *vibrant* canvases filled with color harmonies. In New Mexico, she discovered new themes to inspire her: the reddish *contours* of the mountains, the flame-tinted spikes of jimson weed, the curve of an adobe dwelling, and the bleached animal bones retrieved from the desert.

Every summer for almost two decades, O'Keefe traveled to New Mexico, either renting a house or staying with friends such as Luhan or writer D. H. Lawrence. In 1940 she purchased the old Ghost Ranch. About five years later, she acquired an abandoned adobe

---

1929年，应作家梅布尔·道奇·卢汉的邀请，她旧地重游。那儿的风景、光线，最重要的是它的幽静，都与欧姬芙的寡淡性情极为相配。令她成名的油画都是简洁而近乎抽象的画作，描绘了天空风景和花朵，各种和谐的色彩令画布充满活力。在新墨西哥州，她发现了使她产生灵感的新主题：山脉的微红轮廓、火焰色的曼陀罗尖刺、土坯房的曲线和从沙漠上找到的动物白骨。

在近20年的夏季里，欧姬芙都会前往新墨西哥，要么租一处住所，要么与卢汉和作家劳伦斯这样的朋友在一起共度光阴。1940年，她买下

---

solitude *n.* 独居；独处
vibrant *adj.* 充满生气的

taciturn *adj.* 沉默寡言的
contour *n.* 轮廓；外形

compound and some land in nearby Abiquiu. In 1949, three years after the death of her husband, she moved to New Mexico permanently.

O'Keeffe painted for many years, stopping only when she became almost blind. She died in 1986 at the age of 99.

了"老幽灵牧场"。大约五年后,她又在阿比丘附近买下了一座废弃的土坯墙场院和一部分土地。1949年,在丈夫去世三年后,她搬到新墨西哥州永久定居。

欧姬芙常年绘画,直到她几乎失明。她逝世于1986年,享年99岁。

---

compound *n.* 大院;有墙围的场地

19

Benito Mussolini: "He Made the Trains Run on Time"

The Italians called Benito Mussolini Il Duce (ēl doo′ chā), which means "the leader." In 1922 the king of Italy appointed Mussolini prime minister. He then ruled with absolute power until 1943, when he was *purged* from the Fascist Party.

As a young man, Mussolini worked briefly as a teacher, but his interest in politics and

贝尼托·墨索里尼："他使火车准时运行"

意大利人称贝尼托·墨索里尼为"领导"。1922年，意大利国王任命墨索里尼为总理。之后，他全权统治着意大利，直到1943年被清除出法西斯党。

年轻时，墨索里尼曾短期做过教师，但他对政治的兴趣和写作天赋

---

purge *v.* 清除

a gift for writing led him to *journalism*. His articles were known for their scathing criticism of the Italian government. When Italy entered World War I in 1915, he was *drafted* into the Italian army.

After the war, he founded the Italian Combat League. These were armed groups whose members soon became known as Fascists after the Italian word for "league". The first Fascists were mostly war *veterans*. Many of them were out of work, and all of them were unhappy with the way Italy was being run. Mussolini denounced the government in impassioned speeches at large gatherings. He also condemned the ideas of other political parties. Meanwhile his Fascists, the "Black Shirts" (called that because of their clothing), terrorized both civilians and government officials. Wealthy

---

使他成了一名记者。他的文章因对意大利政府的严厉批评而闻名。1915年，意大利参加第一次世界大战后，他应征加入意大利军队。

战后，他创建了意大利战斗联盟。这个武装组织的成员很快成了恶名昭彰的法西斯分子，法西斯由意大利语中的"联盟"一词而来。第一批法西斯大都是战争退伍军人。他们当中多数人都是失业者，且对意大利的统治方式心怀不满。墨索里尼在大型集会中用激烈的言辞公开抨击政府，还谴责其他政党的理念。同时，他的法西斯分子们，"黑衫党"（因穿着得名），既让平民人心惶惶也让政府高官无安宁之日。富有的商人和地主支

---

journalism *n.* 新闻工作　　　　　　　　　　draft *v.* 征召……入伍
veteran *n.* 退伍军人

businessmen and landowners supported fascism by hiring Black Shirts both for protection and as workers on farms and in factories.

When it seemed that the Fascist Party was about to overturn the government completely, powerful groups, including business interests and the military, *convinced* the king that fascism would bring order to this very disorganized country. Mussolini ruled through the force of his personality and was glorified at huge public *rallies*, on the radio, and in newspaper stories. He also ruled through violence, sending his secret police to deal with people who opposed him.

Did the Fascist Party in fact bring order to Italy? One could say that it brought a certain kind of order, but the efficiency of the Fascist regime was a myth invented partly by Mussolini himself. To this day,

---

持法西斯，他们雇用黑衫党党徒做农场或工厂的工人，藉此方式来作为他们利益的保护伞。

当法西斯党似乎要完全推翻政府时，包括企业界和军队在内的权势集团说服国王相信法西斯主义可以整顿这个极端混乱的国家。墨索里尼以他的飞扬跋扈专制着这个国家，并在大型群众集会上、电台里、报纸的报道中得到美化。他也利用暴力进行统治，派遣秘密警察去处置那些他的反对者。

法西斯党真的整顿了意大利吗？有人可能说它带来了某种秩序，但法

---

convince *v.* 说服   rally *n.* 集会

however, some people still refer to him as the man who "made Italy's trains run on time."

Mussolini's downfall began when he tried to create an Italian empire. He *invaded* Ethiopia and Albania and allied himself with Germany's Adolf Hitler. Within only a few years, hardships at home and defeats abroad led to his *ouster* from the Fascist Party and his imprisonment. His ally, Hitler, sent soldiers to free Mussolini. However, just days before the end of World War II in Europe, he was recaptured and executed.

西斯政权高效的神话，部分是由墨索里尼本人虚构的。然而，直到今天，有些人还称呼他为"使火车准时运行"的人。

当墨索里尼竭力去创造一个意大利帝国时，他的统治开始摇摇欲坠了。他入侵埃塞俄比亚和阿尔巴尼亚，并与德国的阿道夫·希特勒结盟。在短短几年里，国内的经济困境和国外的军事失败，使他被清除出党并被监禁。他的盟友——希特勒，派兵解救了墨索里尼。然而，就在第二次世界大战在欧洲即将结束的前夕，他被重新逮捕并被处决了。

---

invade *v.* 侵略

ouster *n.* 驱逐；撤职

20

What Is Fascism?

Fascism is a form of government in which the needs of the state are thought to outweigh the rights of citizens. Under fascism, freedoms are *suppressed* so that order can be maintained. Change is discouraged. A fascist government controls almost all aspects of life. Such a government, one might say, is the exact

什么是法西斯主义？

法西斯主义是一种置国家的需要于公民权利之上的政府形式。法西斯主义制度下，为确保维持秩序，自由受镇压，改革受阻拦。法西斯政府控制着近乎生活的各个方面。有人可能说，这样的政府恰恰是民主的对立。它强调民族主义和种族认同，不相信其他文化；主张军

---

suppress *v.* 镇压；压制

opposite of democracy. It stresses nationalism and racial identity and regards other cultures with distrust. It is *militaristic* in outlook and quick to declare war.

The Italian ruler Benito Mussolini is credited with the creation of fascism. When World War I ended in 1918, he founded an organization called the Italian Combat League. The word fascism comes from the Italian word fascio, or "league," which in turn comes from the Latin word fasces. The fasces, a bundle of sticks bound tightly together, was a symbol of ancient Rome, whose empire spread from Italy about 2,000 years ago.

Fascism may appeal to those whose lives are in *turmoil*. When existence is a struggle, when there is constant fear of *imminent*

国主义思想，动辄挑起战争。

意大利独裁者，贝尼托·墨索里尼为创建法西斯主义立下头功。1918年，一战刚一结束，他就建立了一个叫做"意大利战斗联盟"的组织。"法西斯主义"一词源于意大利语单词fascio，意为"联盟"，而该词又源于拉丁语单词fasces。fasces意指一束紧捆的木棍，象征约两千年前由意大利向外扩张的古罗马帝国。

法西斯主义往往会蛊惑那些生活在动乱中的人们。当存在成为一种斗

---

militaristic *adj.* 军国主义的　　　　　　　　turmoil *n.* 混乱；骚乱
imminent *adj.* 即将发生的

or sudden attack, fascism may appear to be the solution to all problems. Since the end of World War II in 1945, fascist groups have been created in countries throughout the world, but few have succeeded in *acquiring* any lasting significant influence in their governments.

争，当人们对迫在眉睫的进攻或突然的进攻感到持久恐惧时，法西斯主义也许是解决一切问题的途径。自从1945年二战结束后，世界上出现了很多法西斯团体，但几乎没有哪个能对它们的政府产生任何持久而有意义的影响。

---

acquire *v.* 获得

21

The Roaring Twenties

The decade of the 1920s was like no other period that Americans of the time could imagine. World War I—the "war to end all wars"—had just *concluded*, and the world seemed suddenly a much smaller place. The stock market grew at an *astonishing* rate. Everyone seemed to have plenty of money to spend and plenty of

咆哮的20年代

20世纪20年代一样让当代美国人充满了无限想象。第一次世界大战——这一场结束所有战争的战争——刚刚结束，世界似乎突然小了许多。股票市场以令人瞠目的速度发展，人人似乎都有大笔金钱消费，并有大量闲暇享受生活。称作"轻佻女郎"的姑娘们，舍弃了母

---

conclude *v.* 结束   astonishing *adj.* 令人惊讶的

leisure time in which to enjoy it. Girls known as "flappers" abandoned the modest styles embraced by their mothers for scandalous fashions that included silk stockings, knee-length *hemlines*, bobbed hair, and cosmetics. Young men vied to see who could sit atop a flagpole the longest or who could swallow the largest number of live goldfish.

Indeed, it seemed that the Roaring Twenties howled with *exuberance*, daring, and a devotion to all that was "modern." However, the period could just as accurately be called the Decade of Paradox. Although it was a time of prosperity and enormous social and cultural change, it was also a time of class conflict and oppression.

The United States remained in many ways the land of opportunity,

---

亲钟爱的端庄风格，选择了丝袜、及膝裙、短发和化妆品等使人反感的时尚装扮。年轻的小伙子们比试谁能在旗杆上坐的时间最长，或谁能可以吞下最多的活金鱼。

的确，兴旺的20年代似乎咆哮出人们的高昂热情、勇敢无畏和对一切"现代化"事物的情有独钟。然而，这个时期只能被准确地称作"矛盾的十年"。尽管它是一个繁荣的、有庞大社会与文化变革的时代，同时也是一个充满阶级斗争和压迫的时代。

很大程度上，美国仍然保持机遇之邦这一美名，但它已不再对移民

---

leisure *n.* 空闲时间   hemline *n.* （衣裙的）底边，下摆

exuberance *n.* 热情洋溢；兴高采烈

but it no longer welcomed immigrants. Workers worried that *impoverished* new arrivals would take away their jobs. Wealthy businessmen worried that "un-American" ideas about workers' rights might erode their power and reduce their profits. The government pursued an *isolationist* course and enacted legislation that dramatically reduced the number of foreign-born immigrants permitted to enter the country.

The decade brought mixed blessings for women and families also. Although the Nineteenth Amendment to the Constitution granted women the right to vote in 1920, the Supreme Court overturned progress achieved in minimum-wage and child-labor laws. In 1929 the government withdrew its support for health programs that were intended to help children and pregnant women living in rural regions

---

伸出欢迎之臂了。工人们担心，一贫如洗的新来者会抢走他们的工作；富商担心，工人权利的"非美国式"方案会削弱他们的权力和减少他们的利润。政府则一味贯彻孤立主义方针，议会通过法律，规定要大量减少异国出生移民入境数量。

　　这十年给妇女与儿童带来了什么，也可说是喜忧参半。尽管1920年第十九条美国宪法修正案赋予了妇女选举权，但最高法院撤消了已有所进展的关于最低工资法和童工法方面的议案。1929年，政府撤回了准备帮

---

impoverished *adj.* 贫困的　　　　　　　　　　　isolationist *adj.* 孤立主义的

of the country.

An *energized* Ku Klux Klan in the South terrorized African Americans, Catholics, Jews, and immigrants. The wealth so evident in the industrialized North was notably absent in rural areas, especially in black communities. Poverty drove millions of African Americans to the North and the West in search of jobs, and the *influx* of people into cities such as New York, Detroit, and St. Louis was not without problems. These places, however, also became famous as the centers of a vibrant culture created by African American artists, writers, and musicians who were among the greatest talents of the era.

助农村地区儿童和孕妇的医疗保健计划。

三K党，一个在美国南部的嚣张的恐怖组织，采取恐怖手段迫害美国黑人、天主教徒、犹太人和移民。工业化的北方明显富裕，而农村和黑人区却严重贫困。贫困驱使数百万美国黑人赴北部和西部寻求工作，涌入纽约、底特律和圣路易斯等城市的人们也要解决就业问题。然而，这些城市因拥有各种文化中心而闻名，而创造这种生机勃勃文化的那些人，正是这个时代汇聚在这些城市里的一批极具天赋的非裔美国艺术家、作家和音乐家。

energize *v.* 使活跃；使精力充沛　　　　　influx *n.* （人或物的）大量涌入

22

Vaudeville: Entertainment for All People

The style of entertainment known as *vaudeville* began in the years following the Civil War and increased in popularity after 1900. Almost any kind of act could be found on stage—singers, musicians, *acrobats*, *jugglers*, comics, magicians, and trained animals. Vaudeville acts traveled from town to town, and

歌舞杂耍表演：全民娱乐

以歌舞杂耍表演而著称的娱乐形式始于美国内战后的岁月，并在1900年后名声鹊起。几乎所有行当的演员都会出现在舞台上——歌手、音乐家、杂技演员、杂耍表演者、喜剧演员、魔术师以及受过训练的动物。歌舞杂耍演员们在城镇之间穿梭，全国各地的雇主都建造

vaudeville *n.* 杂耍
juggler *n.* 玩杂耍表演者

acrobat *n.* 杂技演员

entrepreneurs across the country built plush new theaters to attract the best talent.

Vaudeville was a *lucrative* business that made many of the acts and theater owners rich. By 1928 about two million people a day attended performances somewhere in the United States. The reason vaudeville was so popular was that it was affordable, accessible, and appropriate for all ages. One did not have to be rich to buy a ticket nor intellectual to enjoy the show. This form of entertainment, moreover, was apposite for the whole family. More-"adult" acts were confined to another form of theater, called burlesque.

Vaudeville, like so many American businesses, fell on hard times after the crash of the stock market in 1929. By the end of the 1930s,

新式豪华剧院来吸引最有才能的人。

歌舞杂耍表演是一桩有利可图的生意，它使许多演员和剧场老板变得富有。到1928年，在美国某地每天大约有200万人观看表演。歌舞杂耍表演如此受欢迎的原因在于它票价低、易理解并适合所有年龄段的人。人们不用花太多的钱就能买一张票，也不用太聪明就能欣赏表演。此外，这种娱乐形式也适合全家一起观看。更适合"成年"观看的表演只限于在另一类叫"滑稽歌舞杂剧"的剧场上演。

和美国的许多行业一样，歌舞杂耍表演在1929年的股市风暴后陷入

---

entrepreneur *n.* 创业者　　　　　　　　　　lucrative *adj.* 获利丰厚的

vaudeville acts had been replaced by new forms of entertainment, including radio and motion pictures. A number of artists who entered show business through vaudeville went on to have long careers in film, radio, and television.

困境。到20世纪30年代末，歌舞杂耍表演已被包括广播和电影在内的新型娱乐形式取替。很多通过歌舞杂耍表演进入演艺行业的艺人转入到电影、广播和电视娱乐圈中重续演艺生涯。

23

Imperial Russia: The Romanovs and Feudalism

The historical period known as "Imperial Russia" belonged primarily to the *dynasty* of the Romanovs, which ruled from 1613 to 1917. It was under the Romanovs that the Russian Empire reached its height and, for a time, extended from Europe to Asia, across more than a sixth of Earth's surface.

俄罗斯帝国：罗曼诺夫家族和封建制度

历史上称为"俄罗斯帝国"的时期主要是指1613至1917年间的罗曼诺夫王朝。在罗曼诺夫家族的统治下，俄罗斯帝国达到了强盛的顶峰，并一度将其版图从欧洲扩展到亚洲，横跨了超过地球六分之一的面积。

---

dynasty *n.* 王朝

The culture of imperial Russia was feudal, and each tsar, or ruler, held the title Emperor and Autocrat of all Russia. Laws passed in 1649 *wrested* power from the boyars, the wealthy aristocrats, by demanding their allegiance to the tsar. To secure their compliance, the boyars were given large properties and permanent control over the peasants who resided there. These peasants, or *serfs*, and their children were technically property; and when the land was sold or inherited, the serfs were part of the transaction.

Serfs did, however, have a few nominal rights. Property owners were not allowed to kill or injure their serfs, although they could authorize severe punishments that included whippings. Early *legislation* also established the number of days that serfs had to work for their owners. During the fifteenth century, for example, one day's

---

俄罗斯帝国文化属封建性质，每任沙皇或统治者都拥有皇帝或俄罗斯君主的头衔。1649年通过的法律剥夺了富有贵族——波雅尔的权力，藉此要求他们效忠沙皇。为获得波雅尔的服从，君主册封给波雅尔大量房宅地产，并使他们获有对封地内居住农民的永久控制权。严格来说，封地内的农民或农奴及其子女都属于波雅尔的财产，当封地出售或继承时，农奴也是交易的一部分。

然而，农奴确实获有一些名义上的权利。尽管波雅尔对农奴可动用笞刑一类的严刑，但他们不得杀死或伤害农奴。早期的法律还规定了农奴需要为主人做工的天数。比方说，在15世纪，农奴每周有一天的劳动所获

---

wrest *v.* 攫取；抢夺　　　　　　　　　　　　　　serf *n.* 农奴
legislation *n.* 立法

labor each week belonged to the property owner. In the seventeenth century, serfs labored for their owners for three days out of seven. Men and women shared these obligations, and their children were expected to start working by age 14. The laws were enforced *erratically*, however, and a serf's existence was often governed by the owner's *whims*. Serfs could also be assigned to jobs as household servants, laborers in mines or factories, or even soldiers.

In fact, in Imperial Russia it was virtually impossible for people to abandon their homes and find a different and, one would hope, better existence. Serfs were not allowed to leave the property to which they were bound; if they left, they became *fugitives* from the law. Peasants residing on state-owned land faced the same

---

要归属于他们的主人。在17世纪，农奴每周为他们的主人劳动三天。男子与妇女分担这些义务，他们的子女从14岁起就得开始劳动。然而，这些法律未能稳定地执行，一个农奴能否活命往往由主人的一时兴致来决定。农奴们也可能被指派到家中做家仆，到矿山或工厂做劳工，甚至到军队里服役。

事实上，俄罗斯帝国时期，人们几乎不可能离开他们的家庭，以寻求某种符合个人愿望的美好与不同的人生。农奴们不得离开束缚他们的封

---

erratically *adv.* 不定地；不规则地   whim *n.* 突发的念头

fugitive *n.* 逃亡者

obligations as serfs belonging to the boyars. The small middle class of skilled *artisans* and tradespeople had to pay a variety of taxes and similarly were forbidden to change their place of residence. The entire population, even the boyars, was subject to special taxes and was obligated to enlist in the military in times of need.

For more than 200 years, the Romanovs prevented or suppressed rebellion by restricting the Russian people's *mobility* and choices, but serfdom was eventually abolished in 1861.

地；一旦离开，他们就变成了法律上的逃犯。居住在国有土地上的农民会面对与属于波雅尔的农奴相同的义务。由技术工人和商人组成的小、中产阶级必须缴纳各种各样的赋税，还被强令禁止更换居所。全体人民，甚至是波雅尔，都需缴纳特种赋税，并有义务在战争需要时候服兵役。

二百多年来，罗曼诺夫家族通过限制俄罗斯人的流动性和选择权来阻止或镇压叛乱。1861年，农奴制最终被废除。

---

artisan *n.* 手艺人　　　　　　　　　　mobility *n.* 流动性；移动性

24

Peter I and Catherine II: The Westernization of Russia

Europe in the late 1600s and 1700s was the center of science, trade, and the arts. Russia *lagged* far behind in these areas. One tsar and one tsarina from the Romanov family, however, instigated changes that won Russia the respect of its neighbors to the west.

Peter I—called Peter the Great—

彼得一世和叶卡特琳娜二世：俄罗斯的西化

17世纪末至18世纪，欧洲堪称是当时世界的科学、贸易和艺术的中心。俄罗斯在上述领域中还远远落后。然而，由罗曼诺夫家族的一位沙皇和一位女沙皇所发起的变革，使俄罗斯赢得了从其邻邦到西方各国的尊重。

彼得一世，亦称彼得大帝，9岁登基，1682年—1725年期间，执掌

---

lag *v.* 落后

ascended the throne at the age of nine and ruled from 1682 to 1725. As a man, he was tall, strong, and intelligent, but he was nearly *illiterate*. He pursued his own interests in military matters and engineering, and he dedicated himself to the study of European culture. Peter built the seaport city of St. Petersburg to increase trade with other countries. He transformed the *ineffectual* Russian army into a trained force and created the first Russian navy. He also reorganized the government, rewarding people for their accomplishments.

Catherine II—known as Catherine the Great—was the daughter of a German prince. She was far more intelligent and capable than her husband, Peter III. In fact, when he became emperor in 1762,

---

俄罗斯政权。他，身材高大、体格健壮、聪慧过人，但几乎目不识丁。他不懈地发展自己对军事和工程设计方面的兴趣，并全心致力于学习欧洲文化。为扩大与其他国家的贸易往来，彼得建造了海港城市圣彼得堡。他将低效无能的俄罗斯军队彻底改变成了一支训练有素的队伍，创建了第一支俄罗斯海军；他还重组了政府，对为国家做出重大贡献者予以奖励。

叶卡特琳娜二世，以叶卡特琳娜大帝闻名于世，是德国一位亲王的女儿。与她的丈夫彼得三世相比，她更聪明也更有能力。事实上，当丈夫于1762年成为皇帝后，她就曾密谋策划推翻彼得三世的政权。作为俄罗斯

---

illiterate *adj.* 文盲的   ineffectual *adj.* 无能的；无效的

she *conspired* to overthrow him. She reigned 34 years as empress of Russia, during which time she founded several schools—including a teachers' college. She built hospitals and supported medical research. Her vast art collection today is housed in the Hermitage Museum in St. Petersburg.

女皇，她执政俄罗斯达34年之久。在位期间，她创立了几所学校，其中一所是师范学院。她创建医院并支持医学研究。如今，她所收藏的大量艺术品都珍藏在圣彼得堡市的冬宫博物馆。

conspire *v.* 密谋

25

Beyond the Factory: Child Labor in the Cities

At the beginning of the nineteenth century, factory owners faced few *restrictions* on the way they ran their businesses. About one-third of their workers were children between the ages of 7 and 12. Gradually laws intended to develop standards for working children came into being.

工厂之外：城市里的童工

19 世纪初，工厂主们在工厂管理方式上未面临诸多限制。他们雇佣的工人当中约有三分之一是7到12岁的儿童。逐渐地，旨在于描述童工劳动标准的法规开始形成。

---

restriction *n.* 限制

The first child-labor laws were enacted at the state level and usually focused on both *compulsory* education and determining a minimum age for employment. Subsequent laws limited the length of the workday for children. Pennsylvania, for example, limited the workday to 10 hours for children under 12. However, government officials expended *negligible* energy on ensuring that businesses complied with the law. In fact one group of children was left entirely unprotected by labor laws—the children of immigrant families.

By the beginning of the twentieth century, finishing work provided employment for significant numbers of women, particularly those who had recently arrived in the United States. This type of work, also called piecework, was *predominantly* women's work and a mainstay

---

童工劳动法规最初由州一级政府制定，通常注重义务教育和限定受雇佣人的最小年龄。随后的法规限定了儿童工作日的长度。例如，宾夕法尼亚州将12岁以下儿童的工作日限定为10小时。然而，在确保企业遵守这些法规方面，国家公务员们所付出的努力却微乎其微。事实上，有一批来自于移民家庭的儿童，没有得到这些劳动法规的完全保护。

到20世纪初，织物精加工业给大批妇女，尤其是刚到美国的妇女提供了就业机会。这类工作，亦称计件工作，大都由女性从事，是服装产业

---

compulsory *adj.* 强制性的   negligible *adj.* 微不足道的
predominantly *adv.* 主导性地

of the garment industry. Women sewed baby dresses or men's neckties from precut pieces of fabric and made the artificial flowers used to decorate hats. Piecework turned homes into factories that were *exempt* from the law, and countless children worked long hours alongside their mothers and older sisters.

Manufacturers exploited the system shamelessly and paid the lowest wages they could. *Embroidering* a silk dress, which was a 10-day job, might generate a five-dollar payment. There was also the activity called "willowing," in which workers added more strands to ostrich feathers used on hats to make them longer, fuller, and more graceful. The first willowers were paid 15 cents per inch, but a few months later, the pay was reduced to 13 cents. Within three years, willowers were earning only three cents per inch.

的支柱。妇女用预先裁剪好的布料缝制婴儿服装或男人的领带，并制作用于装饰帽子的假花。计件工作把家变成了不受法律约束的工厂，跟母亲和姐姐一起长时间做工的儿童真是数不胜数。

生产商把这种体制利用到极致，支付最低工资，丝毫不知道廉耻。绣制一件真丝连衣裙，女工要干10天活，却只能拿到五美元酬金。还有一项工作叫"捻线"，工人们将线捻到装饰帽子的鸵鸟羽毛上，使羽毛看上去更长、更丰满且更优美。最早的捻线工每英寸会赚到15美分，但几个月以后，这个工资降到了13美分。不到3年，捻线工每英寸就只能赚3美分了。

---

exempt *v.* 免除　　　　　　　　　　　　　embroider *v.* 绣

In order to survive under these circumstances, pieceworkers had even their youngest children help them. In one Italian neighborhood, a threeyear-old girl helped her mother sew clothes, and a pair of sisters left school at three o'clock in the afternoon, only to make artificial flowers at home until nine or ten o'clock at night. In another instance, a child of eight who had lived in New York for three years had never been to school at all and could speak almost no English because all she did was work. Slowly childlabor laws brought these *abuses* to an end.

为能在这样的环境下生存，计件工甚至会让家中最年幼的孩子帮他们干活。在某意大利人街区，一个3岁的小女孩帮妈妈缝衣服，两个姐姐每天下午3点放学，结果一进家就得帮妈妈做假花，一直做到晚上九十点钟。再如，一个在纽约生活了3年的8岁儿童，从未到学校念过一天书，几乎不会讲英语，因为她每天都在干活。慢慢地，童工法结束了这些对儿童的虐待。

abuse *n.* 虐待

26

Vachel Lindsay: Poet for Ordinary People

As the nineteenth century ended, the issue of child labor was part of a general concern about the problems faced by working people. Many publications were filled with articles *decrying* the abuse of child workers in factories, on farms, and in homes. Poets and novelists also bore witness to the poverty, hopelessness, and

韦切尔·林赛：平民诗人

19世纪末，童工问题已经是劳动人民普遍关注的问题之一。许多出版物里写满了谴责工厂、农场和家中虐待童工的文章。诗人和小说家们也证实：贫穷、绝望和无助是20世纪初生活在美国无数童

---

decry *v.* （强烈）批评

helplessness that was the lot of countless child workers living in the United States at the beginning of the twentieth century.

Vachel Lindsay, born in Illinois in 1879, was an artist, poet, and something of a vagabond. Lindsay first traveled through the country in 1906, reciting his poems in exchange for dinner or a place to stay. Poetry, for him, was a kind of storytelling, a spreading of the *"gospel of beauty"*. He regarded poetry as the traditional (and spiritual) art form of ordinary people. Lindsay's poems are musical, and his performances were *dramatic* and full of gesture and movement.

Lindsay's sympathies lay always with the poor, the helpless,

工的命运写照。

1879年，韦切尔·林赛出生于伊利诺斯州。他是一名艺术家、诗人和某种意义上的流浪汉。1906年，林赛首次游历全国，途中以背诵自己创作的诗来换取一顿晚餐或一临时住处。对他来说，诗歌是一种讲故事的方式，是美好福音的传播。他把诗歌视为是普通民众传统（和精神）的艺术形式。林赛的诗悦耳动听，他的诗朗诵表演颇具戏剧化，各种手势和表演动作贯穿其中。

林赛一生始终同情穷苦者、无助者和受压迫者。在1915年发表的一

gospel *n.* 福音　　　　　　　　　　　　dramatic *adj.* 戏剧的

and the *oppressed*. In a poem published in 1915, he describes the despair of children forced to work, calling them "the leaden-eyed." Lindsay *enumerates* their sufferings—starvation, endless labor, and an existence often without meaning.

Lindsay's life was beset by difficulties. Despite publication in Poetry magazine and his performing before President Woodrow Wilson, in the 1930s his reputation went into decline.

首诗中，他描述了被强迫劳作的儿童们的内心绝望，称其为"呆滞的目光"。林赛列举了他们所受的苦难——饥饿、无休止的劳作和通常无意义的存在。

尽管林赛在《诗歌》杂志上发表作品，并为伍德罗·威尔逊总统表演过诗朗诵，但在20世纪30年代，他的声誉开始下降。他的的一生充满了艰辛和坎坷。

oppressed *n.* 被压迫者　　　　　　　　enumerate *v.* 列举；枚举

27

Opera: The Basics

The ancient art of opera can be brilliant entertainment; it is a mixture of music, drama, and sometimes dance, staged with *elaborate* sets and costumes. Opera is often unappreciated by many, however, partly because of some of the *stereotypes* associated with it. Some of its critics say that the narratives are too

歌剧的基本要素

歌剧这门古老艺术是一种辉煌而杰出的娱乐形式；它是音乐、戏剧、有时还有舞蹈和精心设计过场景和服装的舞台的组合。然而，很多人并不欣赏歌剧，部分原因是由于某些与其相关的俗套。有些批评者说它的叙述太过复杂。也有人抱怨歌剧不易理解，因为歌剧经常用外

---

elaborate *adj.* 复杂的；周密的   stereotype *n.* 模式化形象

MCGRAW-HILL

complex. Others complain that operas cannot be understood because they are often performed in foreign languages. Stereotypes aside, opera is an art form enjoyed by many music lovers. Operas can be comedies or tragedies or stories taken from history.

The story of an opera is generally simple so as to avoid *distracting* the audience from the music. The *libretto*, or script, sets each scene and describes the action in both words and stage directions. The music of an opera—the way it advances the action and the feelings it inspires in the listeners—is particularly important. The three principal musical elements are the *overture* (including interludes—miniovertures between acts), the recitative, and the aria.

The overture is the instrumental introduction to the opera, the

---

语表演。撇开俗套不谈，歌剧是一种受许多音乐爱好者喜爱的艺术形式。歌剧可以是喜剧或悲剧，也可能来源于历史故事。

一部歌剧的故事情节通常很简单，为的是避免分散观众对音乐的注意。歌剧剧本或脚本，设定了每个情景并用语言和舞台指示来描述剧情细节。一部歌剧的音乐——推动情节和激发听众情感的方式——尤为重要。三个最重要的音乐要素是序曲（包括插曲和两幕之间的小序曲）、宣叙调和咏叹调。

序曲是歌剧的器乐引言，它的用途随着时间而变化。19世纪时，序

---

distract *v.* 分散（注意力）；使分心   libretto *n.* （歌剧或音乐剧的）歌词
overture *n.* （歌剧、戏剧等的）序曲

purpose of which has *evolved* over time. During the nineteenth century, the overture began to combine *snippets* of melodies from arias, ballets, and other musical elements in a medley of the opera's musical themes.

A *recitative* is less a song than a monologue that is sung rather than spoken. A recitative is an element, older than the overture, that was invented at the beginning of the seventeenth century as a means of telling a story in music; the first operas were actually a series of recitatives joined by musical *interludes*. Because an opera is basically a play set to music, the recitative is a means of telling the audience what is going on and what is about to happen.

An aria is a solo performance—often one of the highlights of the

曲已开始把咏叹调、芭蕾舞曲和其他音乐元素的片段结合到歌剧主题乐之中。

宣叙调与其说是演员唱出来的歌曲不如说是演员念出来的独白。它发明于17世纪初，作为一种在音乐中讲述故事的手段，是一个比序曲更古老的元素；最早的歌剧其实是用音乐插曲连接起来的一系列宣叙调。由于一部歌剧基本上是一种由音乐设定情景的戏剧，宣叙调是将正在进行和将要发生的戏情内容告诉给观众的一种手段。

咏叹调为独唱表演——经常是歌剧的一个高潮。咏叹调可以是爱的宣

evolve *v.* 进化；逐步发展　　　　　　　snippet *n.* 片段
recitative *n.* 宣叙调　　　　　　　　　 interlude *n.* 间歇

opera. Arias can be declarations of love or expressions of hope, happiness, sorrow, or anguish. Many composers have written *arias* to showcase the vocal gifts of singers; some *sopranos* were indeed famous for the very high notes that they could sing. Arias are not the only songs in opera, however. Duets, compositions for three or four voices, and large-group numbers (choruses) are also common. These diverse musical elements, combined with visual elements in costumes and sets as well as the dramatic content of the story, make the opera the complex art form that it is.

言，也可以是希望、快乐、悲伤或痛苦的表达。许多作曲家设计咏叹调来展现歌手的歌唱天赋；有些女高音歌手实际上是因为她们可以唱出的超高音而出名。然而，咏叹调并不是歌剧中仅有的歌曲。三四种声音组合而成的重奏和很多人的大合唱也很常见。各种各样的音乐元素，与服装和布景等视觉要素及故事的戏剧化情节结合在一起，使歌剧成了一种复杂的艺术形式。

aria *n.* 咏叹调 soprano *n.* 女高音

28

Madam Butterfly and Miss Saigon

Through the centuries, artists have told stories through song. In 1904 Italian composer Giacomo Puccini created an opera based on the story "Madame Butterfly". Set in Japan, the opera is a *poignant* narrative of loyalty, *deception*, and cultural differences.

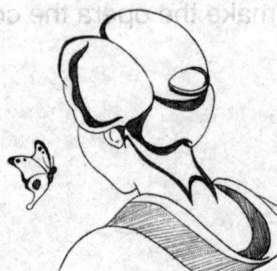

A Japanese woman, Cio-Cio-San,

《蝴蝶夫人》和《西贡小姐》

几个世纪以来，艺术家们通过歌曲来讲述故事。1904年，意大利作曲家贾科莫·普契尼根据"蝴蝶夫人"的故事编创了一部歌剧。歌剧以日本为背景，叙述了一段有关忠诚、欺骗和文化差异的辛酸故事。

一个名为巧巧桑的日本女人嫁给了一个叫做平克顿的美国中尉。对平

---

poignant *adj.* 辛酸的   deception *n.* 欺骗；受骗

marries an American, Lieutenant Pinkerton. To Pinkerton the marriage is *revokable*; he abandons Cio-Cio-San and marries an American woman. When Pinkerton returns to Japan, he discovers that Cio-Cio-San has born a son. He takes the child from her; and Cio-Cio-San, overcome with grief, takes her own life. The opera contains an *exquisite* aria in which Cio-Cio-San expresses her love for Pinkerton and her hope that "one fine day" they will be together.

Miss Saigon, first performed in 1989, is a musical loosely based on the opera Madam Butterfly. Set in the final days of the Vietnam War, it brings together Kim, who lives in poverty in Saigon, and Chris, an American soldier. In 1975 the two are separated. Back in the

克顿来说，这是一桩随时可以取消的婚姻；他抛弃了巧巧桑并娶了一个美国女人。当平克顿回到日本，他发现巧巧桑为他生了一个儿子。他把儿子从她身边带走了；巧巧桑悲伤欲绝，以自尽方式了结了一生情缘。歌剧包含了一段优美的咏叹调，其中巧巧桑表达了她对平克顿的挚爱和 "终有一天" 他们将能在一起的期望。

1989年，《西贡小姐》首次上演，是一部没严格根据歌剧《蝴蝶夫人》改编的音乐剧。该剧以越南战争的最后岁月为背景，住在西贡贫困

revokable *adj.* 可撤销的；能取消的   exquisite *adj.* 精美的

United States, Chris marries; when he *revisits* Asia a few years later, he learns that he has a son, Tam. Kim wants Chris to take Tam back to the United States with him so that Tam will have an opportunity for a good life. Chris wants the child to remain with Kim, so Kim kills herself to ensure Tam's future.

区的金和一个叫做克里斯的美国士兵结合在了一起。1975年，他们分开了。回到美国后，克里斯结了婚；当几年后重返越南，他发现自己有了一个叫做塔姆的儿子。金想让克里斯带塔姆一起回美国，这样塔姆就有机会过一种好的生活。但克里斯想让这个孩子留在金身边，金为确保塔姆的未来而自尽身亡。

revisit *v.* 重游

29

Medieval Maps: Choosing the Center of the World

The technique of mapmaking, known as *cartography*, today relies upon factual geographical information. Locations are plotted with accuracy, and users can determine where a place is, how far away it is, and how to get there. For the cartographers of the Middle Ages, however, a map was an expression of a religious,

中世纪地图：选定世界的中心

时至今日，以"地图学"著称的地图制作技术依赖于获取真实地理信息。精确地标定出地理位置，地图使用者能够判定某个地方的方位、测定与该地的距离和去该地的方式。然而，对中世纪的绘图者来说，一张地图是一种宗教的表达，而不是对世界的科学勘测。此类中世

---

cartography *n.* 制图法；地图绘制

rather than a scientific, view of the world. These medieval maps of the world, known by their Latin name mappaemundi, generally took one of two *formats*: the "T in O" or the *zonal* layout.

T-in-O maps combined religious beliefs with history and geography. In the medieval world, the most important historical events were the events of the Bible. For Christians the most significant biblical events surrounded the life of Jesus. The layout of a T-in-O map resembles a T inscribed within an O. The circle represents Earth and symbolizes a universal, eternal God. Inside the circle are simple shapes that represent the continents of Europe, Asia, and Africa.

Unlike a modern map, on which the direction north appears at the top, T-in-O maps were oriented to the east. Because the Holy

---

纪世界地图，拉丁名为mappaemundi（意为：世界的粗布），通常采用两种制式中的一种：T-in-O图面或分带图面设计。

　　T-in-O 地图将宗教信仰与历史和地理结合在一起。中世纪最重要的历史事件是圣经事件。对基督徒来说，最有意义的圣经事件是与耶稣的生活紧密联系的。一张T-in-O 设计的地图看似一个T字型内接在一个圆圈里。圆圈代表的是地球并象征万能、永恒的神。圆圈内是代表欧洲、亚洲和非洲大陆的简单形状。

　　与北方在上的现代地图不同，T-in-O 地图的上为东方。因为圣地是

---

format *n.* 程式；格式 　　　　　　　　　　　　　　　**zonal** *adj.* 区域的

Land was the center of the medieval spiritual world, cartographers set Jerusalem and the Christian Holy Lands toward the center and the Garden of Eden of the Bible at the top of the circle. People, places, and events of particular religious significance were located near this "center" of the world. Beings and locations regarded as strange, hostile, or evil were arranged farther away. Distance on the map, therefore, was an illustration of spiritual distance from heaven rather than a representation of geographical distance. On a T-in-O map, Asia forms the *crossbar* of the T; and the Mediterranean Sea, between Europe at the lower left and Africa at the lower right, is the *vertical* stem.

The zonal maps borrowed the ancient Greek idea that Earth was divided into five climate zones. There were two temperate zones,

---

中世纪精神世界的中心，绘图者们将耶路撒冷和基督教圣地设为中心，将圣经中的伊甸园设在圆圈的顶端。有特殊宗教意义的人、地方和事件被定位于这个世界的"中心"。奇怪的、敌意的或邪恶的人和地方被安排在远方。因此，地图距离只表明人间与天堂的精神距离，而不代表地理距离。在T-in-O 地图里，亚洲构成了T的横线；位于左下角的欧洲和右下角的非洲之间的地中海，是垂直的竖线。

分带地图借用了古希腊地球被划分为五个气候带的想法。地球上有两

---

crossbar *n.* 横木   vertical *adj.* 垂直的

where people could live on each side of a hot, uninhabitable region at the *equator*. There were also two freezing areas, at the top and bottom of Earth. Like the T-in-O maps, zonal maps are circular, but usually the direction north appears at the top. Countries, biblical characters, and historical figures are located in the temperate zone above the equator.

In ancient times, the zonal-map form was sometimes *merged* with the T-in-O map, creating an even more complicated representation of the world.

个温带，温带人生活在炎热、不能居住的赤道带两边。在地球的顶部和底部还有两个寒带地区。和T-in-O 地图一样，分带地图的设计也是圆形的，只是通常北方在上。国家、圣经人物和历史人物被定位在赤道以上的温带。

　　古时候，分带地图有时会与T-in-O 地图结合在一起，以组成一个更加复杂的对世界的描绘。

---

equator *n.* 赤道 　　　　　　　　　　　　　　　　merge *v.* 合并

30

The Hereford Map

The Hereford Map, an enormous map of the world about five feet high and four feet wide, is named for its home in the Hereford Cathedral in England. Created at the end of the thirteenth century, it is a combination of Christian belief, historical record, scientific knowledge, superstition, and *folklore*. It is based on information from

赫里福德地图

赫里福德地图是一张巨大的、将近5英尺高和5英尺宽的世界地图，因来自于英国的赫里福德大教堂而得名。制于13世纪末，它是基督教信仰、历史记录、科学知识、迷信和民间传说的结合体。该图

---

folklore *n.* 民间传说；民俗

contemporary encyclopedias of animals, known as bestiaries. It also includes information from texts written a thousand years earlier.

Some of the *diminutive* drawings depict real animals, such as the pelican, rhinoceros, and camel. Some show mythological creatures, such as the phoenix (a bird said to be reborn from its ashes every hundred years), the dragon, and the unicorn. On the Hereford Map, distance often meant strangeness, so the most fantastic beasts were placed on the edges of Africa and Asia, as remote from Europe as possible.

In India—on the eastern *rim* of the world, on this map—an elephant appears as well as the blood-red *manticore* with its human

---

是根据那时的当代动物百科全书《动物寓言集》信息以及早于那时代一千年前的文本资料绘订而成。

　　某些小型的画描绘了真实的动物，比如鹈鹕、犀牛和骆驼。有些展现了神话中的生物，例如凤凰（一种传说每一百年会从灰烬中重生的鸟）、龙和独角兽。赫里福德地图中，距离经常意指陌生程度，所以最荒诞离奇的野兽被放在远离欧洲的非洲和亚洲的边缘地带。

　　在这个地图世界的最东边——印度，有一头大象，还有发出蛇嘘声

---

diminutive *adj.* 微小的　　　　　　　　　　　　　　　　rim *n.* 边沿

manticore *n.* 人头狮身蝎尾兽

face, lion's body, scorpion's tail, and *hissing* serpent's voice. The yale—with its body of a horse, tail of an elephant, and jaws like a goat's—was a *pugnacious* beast with long horns. According to tradition, the combative yale used only one horn as a weapon in battle and folded the other back out of the way.

的、血红色的人头狮身蝎尾怪兽。有一种长着长角的野迻，马身象尾，颌骨类似山羊，生性好斗。根据传统，好斗的野迻在战斗中只用一只角作为武器，将另一只角收拢于不碍事之处。

hiss *v.* 发嘶嘶声   pugnacious *adj.* 好斗的；好战的

31

African Slavery in America: 1600–1865

An enslaved person is one who lives in complete and *involuntary servitude* as the property of another person. Laws have often defined enslaved people as things and not human beings. According to these laws, such property could be bought, sold, traded, given as a gift, or even destroyed. Throughout history, the practice

美国的非洲奴隶制：1600–1865

奴隶是指作为他人财产的、完全处于非自愿奴役状态的人。法律经常将奴隶定义为物品而不是人。依据此类法律，这种财产可以买进、卖出、用来交易、作为礼物，甚至毁掉。纵观历史，实施奴隶制

---

involuntary *adj.* 非自愿的　　　　　　　　　　servitude *n.* 奴役

of slavery has at some point been a major factor in the economy of many societies.

The European trade in enslaved Africans began in the fifteenth century, when Portuguese and Spanish *merchants* started buying African people from African and Arab sellers. Other countries, including England, entered the slave trade during the next 100 years.

African slavery in America's English colonies dates to the seventeenth century, when 20 Africans were bought off a Dutch ship in Jamestown, Virginia. These people, and many who were to follow, were said to be in "limited servitude". In other words, enslaved persons could be freed once the slaveholder felt that they had worked off the money paid for them. The laws that defined limited

是许多社会某阶段经济的一个主要因素。

欧洲的非洲奴隶交易始于15世纪，当时葡萄牙和西班牙商人开始从非洲和阿拉伯奴隶贩子手中购买非洲奴隶。在随后的100年中，包括英国在内的其他国家也开始了奴隶贸易。

美国英属殖民地的非洲奴隶制可追溯到17世纪，当时在弗吉尼亚詹姆斯敦的奴隶贩子将20个非洲奴隶从一条荷兰帆船上买下。这些人和后到来的许多人，被说成是受到"有限的奴役"。换句话说，当奴隶主觉得这些奴隶以做工形式抵消了购买他们所花的费用时，他们就可以获得自由。

merchant *n.* 商人

servitude, however, were vague. Many people in limited servitude remained enslaved for life. By the start of the American Revolution in 1775, most Africans not already freed had become *hereditary* slaves. This meant that their children also were enslaved.

Although the Northern states developed economies based on industry, agriculture remained the main activity in the South. Because of the need for labor on Southern plantations, the number of enslaved Africans brought to the United States increased in the late 1700s. By 1800 almost 900,000 people were enslaved in the United States, but only about 36,000 of them lived in the North. According to the *census* of 1860, one year before the beginning of the Civil War, almost 4,000,000 people were enslaved in the South.

Vermont, in 1777, became the first of the Northern states to put

---

然而，法律对有限奴役的界定非常模糊，许多有限奴役的人终生遭受了奴役。1775年，美国独立战争开始时，大部分还未获得自由的非洲人成了世袭奴隶，这一点意味着，他们的孩子也要遭受奴役。

尽管北方各州以工业为主发展经济，可南方还是以农业为主要的生产活动。18世纪末，南方种植园需要大批劳动力，所以被贩运到美国的非洲奴隶人数大幅增加。到19世纪，美国大约有900 000名奴隶，但其中只有约36 000人生活在北方。根据1860年内战开始前所做的人口调查，南方差不多拥有4 000 000名奴隶。

1777年，佛蒙特成了北方废除奴隶制的第一个州。在18世纪，宾夕

---

hereditary *adj.* 世袭的   census *n.* 人口普查

an end to slavery. Pennsylvania, New York, and Rhode Island began a process of gradual *abolition* in the eighteenth century. An act of the federal government in 1787 outlawed slavery in the Northwest Territory, an area that extended to the Mississippi River. U.S. law *banned* the transportation of enslaved persons from Africa in 1808. Maine joined the Union as a free state in 1820. New Hampshire ended slavery in 1857. Slavery in the border state of Delaware, however, continued until the Thirteenth Amendment went into effect nationwide in 1865, following the end of the Civil War.

法尼亚、纽约和罗德岛开始了逐渐废除奴隶制的进程。1787年，联邦政府一项法案将延伸到密西西比河的西北领地内的蓄奴制度制宣布为非法。1808年，美国法律禁止从非洲运输奴隶。缅因州在1820年作为一个自由州加入了联盟。新汉普郡在1857年结束了奴隶制。然而，位于边境的特拉华州还延续着奴隶制，直到1865年美国内战结束，第十三条修正案在全国生效之后，该州奴隶制终告结束。

abolition *n.* 废除

ban *v.* 明令禁止

32

A Narrative That Helped to Change the World

Olaudah Equiano was born about the year 1745 and lived enslaved until he was able to buy his own freedom in 1766. By the time of his death in 1797, he had become one of the most respected men of his era. He had traveled throughout the world, written his *autobiography*, and earned a place of honor in English society.

为改变奴隶制而终生奋斗

阿罗德·爱克伊诺大约出生于1745年。直到1766年他能用钱赎回人身自由前，他始终过着受奴役的生活。在1797年他临终之前，他已经成为他那一时代最受尊敬的人之一。他环游世界，撰写了自传，并在英国社会赢得了荣誉。

autobiography *n.* 自传

The Interesting Narrative of the Life of Olaudah Equiano was published in 1789. Some scholars question his claim to have been born in Eboe in present-day Nigeria, but the rest of the tale agrees with the historical record. As an enslaved person, Equiano fought in naval battles against the French, alongside his English master. Sold and then resold, he was the victim of *degradation* and a witness to appalling abuses. As a freed man, he joined forces with those working to abolish slavery and converted to Christianity.

During the eighteenth century, a growing number of white people had begun to question the justness of slavery. Many, however, thought that cruelty toward enslaved people was similar to the abuse of animals. Equiano's book helped to change the way white people *perceived* people of color. His *assertion* that all souls are equal before God persuaded many that slavery was more than an act of simple cruelty—it was the worst form of inhumanity.

1789年，《阿罗德·爱克伊诺一生的有趣故事》公开发表。有些学者对他声称自己为现今尼日利亚的伊博族后裔提出质疑，但余下的故事与历史记录相符。作为一个奴隶，爱克伊诺跟随他的英国主人与法国人打过海战。他被卖了又卖，是落魄的受害人和遭受骇人听闻虐待的见证人。作为一个自由人，他联合人们一起为废除奴隶制而工作，并皈依了基督教。

18世纪时，越来越多的白人开始质疑奴隶制的公正性。然而，许多人认为残忍地对待奴隶如同虐待动物。爱克伊诺的书帮助改变了白人对有色人种的看法。他主张上帝面前人人平等，这个主张使许多人相信，奴隶制远远不止是一种简单残暴的行为——而是一种最卑劣的非人道行径。

---

degradation *n.* 堕落　　　　　　　　　　　　perceive *v.* 感知到；认为
assertion *n.* 主张；断言

33

Ellen Swallow Richards and the Science of Home Economics

Ellen Swallow Richards was the first woman to earn a bachelor's degree from the Massachusetts Institute of Technology (MIT). A chemist, social activist, teacher, and first woman member of the Institute of Mining and Metallurgical Engineering, she believed that *housekeeping* was a science. She was

埃伦·斯沃洛·理查兹和家庭经济学

埃伦·斯沃洛·理查兹是从麻省理工学院获得学士学位的第一位女性。身兼化学家、社会活动家、教师和矿冶工程学会第一位女会员等数职，她认为家务管理是一门科学，同时她还是一位女性教育并

---

housekeeping *n.* 料理家务

also a progressive thinker at a time when education for women was not widely encouraged. Women, she thought, needed to learn about money matters and have up-to-date information on cleanliness and *nutrition*. She also believed that education provided the best protection against greedy businesses that focused only on profits or governments that failed to keep water and food supplies safe. She encouraged women from all backgrounds to get the best education possible.

Ellen Swallow was born in 1842 and was brought up in Massachusetts in a family of modest means. A graduate of Vassar College in New York, she returned to New England to attend MIT. After her marriage to Professor Robert H. Richards, she worked in a *laboratory* at MIT, analyzing contamination of water sources in

---

未得到广泛支持时期的进步思想家。她认为,女人应该学会理财并该了解卫生和营养学的最新信息。她还认为,教育为反对只专注于利益的贪婪企业或不能保证水和食品供应安全的政府提供了最好的防护。她鼓励来自于所有不同背景的女性都尽可能地接受最好的教育。

埃伦·斯沃洛出生于1842年,在马萨诸塞州一个中等收入家庭中长大。从纽约瓦萨学院毕业后,她回到新英格兰,就读于麻省理工学院。嫁给一位名为罗伯特·理查兹的教授后,她一直在麻省理工学院的一个实验

---

nutrition *n.* 营养   laboratory *n.* 实验室

Massachusetts. Her work led to that state's creation of the first food-inspection laws. She also focused attention on public *sanitation* and the importance of sanitary sewer-treatment systems. She was instructor at MIT from 1884 until her death in 1911.

Like other progressive thinkers of the era, Richards was concerned about problems of the poor and the effect of the environment, or surroundings, on society. She considered the environment a key factor in quality of life. Within the family, as in the world at large, science was chief in the *arsenal* of weapons used to fight poverty. Science could help to manage finances, keep a home safe and clean, and improve quality of life. Food properly cooked could be tasty, nutritious, and inexpensive. Better and cheaper food could protect the health and improve the lives of working-class families. At

---

室工作，从事马萨诸塞州水源中污染物的分析。她的研究促成了该州第一部食品检查法的诞生。她还关注公共卫生和生活污水处理系统的重要性。自1884年起，她在麻省理工学院任讲师工作，直到1911年去世。

　　和许多那个时代的进步思想家一样，理查兹关心穷人的疾苦，也关心环境对社会的影响。她将环境视为高质量生活的一个核心因素。小到家庭，大到社会，科学是用于战胜贫穷的首要武器；科学可以帮助人们理财；科学可使一个家既安全又整洁并能提高人生质量。合理烹饪的食物应当美味、富有营养且价格便宜。质优价廉的食物可以保护健康并改善工人

---

sanitation *n.* 公共卫生　　　　　　　　　　　arsenal *n.* 武器；军火库

the New England Kitchen in Boston, she served low-cost meals and demonstrated how to prepare them easily.

Richards created the field of *domestic* science, a discipline now called home economics, and *elevated* it to a serious college subject. She worked tirelessly for the addition of these classes to Boston's public schools. Richards was a national leader in developing academic standards, content materials, and teacher training for this new field. Her publications cover a wide range of topics—from the chemistry of cooking and cleaning to the cost of living and conservation by sanitation.

阶级的家庭生活。在波士顿的新英格兰厨房，她为人们端上亲手做的低成本饭菜并示范怎样轻松地做好这类饭菜。

理查兹开创了家政学领域的历史先河，是她把这门现今称作家庭经济学的学科升格为大学讲堂内的一门重点课程。为使波士顿公立学校增设这门课程，她不知疲倦地努力工作。在给这一新领域开拓学术标准、制定课程材料和教师培训等方面，理查兹的科研工作水平在全美国处于领先地位。她的出版物探讨了一系列广泛的论题——从烹饪与清洁的关系到家庭生活和环境卫生保护成本等。

---

domestic *adj.* 家务的；家庭的　　　　　　　　elevate *v.* 提拔；抬高

34

The Association of Collegiate Alumnae: Women and Higher Education

In 1881 the number of women who had graduated from college was small, and those who had achieved this milestone *cherished* the companionship of their *peers*. One autumn 17 of these women gathered for a meeting in Ellen Swallow Richards's chemistry laboratory at the Massachusetts

大学女校友协会：女性和高等教育

1881 年，从大学毕业的女性人数很少，因此凡是有过大学经历的女毕业生都很珍惜她们与同学的同窗之谊。同年秋天，有17名女毕业生在麻省理工学院埃伦·斯沃洛·理查兹化学实验室召开了一次会议。翌年1月，有65位女生在波士顿举行了会议。

---

cherish *v.* 珍爱；珍视   peer *n.* 同龄人

Institute of Technology. In January of the following year, 65 women met in Boston. Their purpose was the creation of a group to support women's education. Marion Talbot, one of the first women to *enroll* at Boston University, described some of the projects she thought they might take on.

The group was called the Association of Collegiate Alumnae (ACA) because they all held college degrees. Its first goal was to improve the access of women to higher education. Members also looked for ways to improve opportunities for women in the workplace. In 1885, for instance, the group published a report that *debunked* the accepted idea that an education was bad for a woman's health. The

---

她们的目的是要创立一个支持女性教育的组织。最早进入波士顿大学的女性之一——马里恩·塔尔博特，描述了她们可能会进行的计划。

这个组织被称为"大学女校友协会"（ACA），因为她们都拥有大学学位。它的第一个目标是提高女性参加高等教育的人数。成员们还想办法增加女性就业的机会。例如1885年，这个组织发表了一份报告来揭穿公认的"教育对一个女性的健康是有害的"这一说法。大学女校友协会致力于

---

enroll v. （使）加入；登记   debunk v. 揭露……的真相

ACA worked to change laws that *restricted* women's rights. It also gave money to women conducting research projects.

Soon women in other cities formed local branches of the ACA. In 1921 the group was renamed the American Association of University Women (AAUW) and set up its national office in Washington, D.C. Today the AAUW has a *membership* of about 150,000.

修改限制女性权利的法律，还为女性从事的研究项目提供大笔资金。

不久，其他城市的女性组成了大学女校友协会的地方分会。1921年，这个组织更名为"美国大学妇女联合会"(AAUW)，并在华盛顿特区设立了它的全国办公室。今天美国大学妇女联合会大约拥有150 000名成员。

---

restrict *v.* 限制　　　　　　　　　membership *n.* 成员身份；成员数

35

The Tour de France

The Tour de France is one of the most *prestigious* and historic races open to professional cyclists. Today, the peloton, as the main body of the competitors is called, *pedals* through approximately 3,000 miles of French countryside. About one million spectators line the tour route each day, and another 50 million people around the world

环法自行车赛

环法自行车赛是面向职业自行车选手的最有声望和最具历史意义的竞赛之一。今天,参赛者的主体——主车群,穿行法国乡村大约3000英里。每天大约有1 000 000观众排列在环行赛道边观赛,另有50 000 000来自世界各地的人观看电视报道。

---

prestigious *adj.* 有声望的   pedal *n.* 踏板

watch televized coverage.

The tour was created as a *gimmick* to generate income for a struggling new French sports magazine. The magazine's cycling reporter, Georges Lefèvre, suggested that the magazine *sponsor* a race. It would last several days and travel through several important towns—in effect, a tour around France by bicycle. Surely, he argued, enthusiasts would rush out to buy every copy of the magazine that provided complete coverage of such an event, and such a magazine would also attract a considerable amount of paid advertising.

Lefèvre's expectations turned out to be justified. On July 1, 1903, 60 riders headed west out of Paris in a clockwise circuit around France. Nineteen days and 1,500 miles later, 21 riders crossed the

---

环法赛，是一家艰难挣扎的新法国运动杂志社把它作为创收噱头而创立的。这家杂志的自行车记者，乔治斯·勒菲弗建议杂志社应该发起一项竞赛，竞赛要持续几天，经过几个重要的城镇——事实上是骑自行车环行法国。不错，他争辩道，自行车爱好者，一定会冲出家门到大街上购买每一本有对赛事做全程报道的杂志，这样的杂志必然还会吸引数目可观的付费广告。

事实证明，勒菲弗的预期实现了。1903年7月1日，60名骑手向西驶出巴黎，绕法国顺时针环行。历时19天共骑行1500英里后，21名骑手返

---

gimmick *n.* 花招　　　　　　　　　　　sponsor *v.* 倡议；赞助

finish line back in Paris.

The *itinerary* of the tour changes from year to year, but the finish line is always in Paris. Each stage of the race offers some particular challenge, including individual and team time trials. There are also arduous climbs through the mountains and *precipitous* downhill sections.

The rules also are adjusted from year to year but in general allow the participation of about 20 teams of nine riders. Individual and team progress is carefully monitored, and the leaders at each stage are privileged to wear special jerseys. The leader with the fastest time overall wears the yellow jersey. The green jersey belongs to the rider who has earned the most points, and the *jersey* with red polka

---

回巴黎冲过了终点线。

环行路线每一年都有所改变，但是终点线一直设在巴黎。竞赛的每一个阶段都安排某一类特殊的挑战赛项，其中包括个人和小组计时赛。选手还要经过艰巨的爬坡段和险峻的下坡段。

规则每一年也会修改，但是通常允许大约20支车队参赛，每队由9名骑手组成。个人和小组的进度都要受到仔细监控，每一阶段的领先者都有权穿上颜色特别的运动衫。总时间最快的领先者要穿黄色领骑衫；得分最多的骑手穿绿色运动衫；山路阶段的表现最好的运动员穿红色带圆点运动

---

itinerary *n.* 旅行计划   precipitous *adj.* 险峻的
jersey *n.* 运动衫

dots signifies the best performance in the mountain stages. There is also a white jersey for the best competitor under the age of 25.

The tour has run annually, since its *inception*, except for the years during World Wars I and II. Each race has featured extraordinary events, triumphs, and tragedies. Since 1910 four riders have lost their lives while on the tour, three of them as a result of injuries suffered in accidents during the race. In 2002 American cyclist Lance Armstrong, who had undergone *surgery* and other treatments for cancer in 1996, won a fourth straight victory in the Tour de France.

衫；25岁以下最优秀的赛车手穿白色运动衫。

除一战和二战期间出现间断外，环法自行车赛自开办起每年举办一次。每次竞赛都对精彩赛事、选手们的凯旋与悲剧经历做出新闻特写。自1910年起，四名选手在环行赛中丧生，其中三人之死是因为竞赛时遭遇意外、伤重身亡。在1996年时为治疗癌症而经历过外科手术和其他疗法的美国选手兰斯·阿姆斯特朗，在2002年环法自行车赛中取得了四连冠。

---

inception *n.* 开始；开端　　　　　　　　　　　surgery *n.* 外科手术

36

A Brief History of the Bicycle

At the end of the eighteenth century, a French gentleman was observed on a two-wheeled *conveyance*, propelling himself by pushing his feet against the ground. Before long, people were *devising* ways to make this primitive bicycle an effective means of transportation.

Although a number of models preceded

自行车简史

18世纪末，人们看到一位法国绅士在一辆有两个轮子的运输工具上，将脚踩向地面来使自己前进。不久以后，人们便构想使这个原始脚踏车成为一种有效的交通工具。

尽管之前有一些模型，1863年制造的"老爷车"，通常被认为是第

---

conveyance *n.* 交通工具   devise *v.* 构思；设计

it, the "boneshaker," built in 1863, is generally considered to be the first successful bicycle. A stiff frame and metal-rimmed wheels produced the unpleasant, jarring ride from which it takes its nickname. Its official name was the *velocipede*.

The next innovation was the highwheeler, a bicycle with an immense front wheel and a small rear wheel. It offered a more comfortable ride than the velocipede, but it was difficult to *mount* and dangerous to operate. In fact, the phrase "take a header" originated as a description of falling head first from the highwheeler's seat.

By the 1880s, however, manufacturers had returned to a design that featured wheels of equal size. They also made bicycles more powerful by connecting the pedals to the rear wheels with a chain.

一辆成功的自行车。呆板的构造和发出令人不愉快刺耳声的金属轮使它获得了这个绰号。它的正式名称是"脚蹬两轮车"。

下一个创新是有着巨大前轮和小后轮的高轮车。它骑起来比脚蹬两轮车舒服,但是它很不容易爬上去,驾驶起来也很危险。事实上,"倒栽葱"这个词就源于对从高轮车的座位上倒栽下来的描述。

然而,到19世纪80年代,生产商们又恢复了两个车轮一样大小的设计。他们还将脚踏板与后轮用一个链子连起来以使自行车有更大的功率。

---

velocipede *n.* 蹬地脚踏车   mount *v.* 骑上;登上

Pushing on the pedals not only made the front wheel go around but *rotated* the rear wheel as well.

Since that time, materials that make a stronger frame, springs and *pneumatic* tires that cushion shocks from the road, and improved safety features have enhanced this basic design.

踩脚踏板不仅会使前轮转动，也同样使后轮旋转。

从那时起，使框架更坚固的材料、缓和地面冲击的弹簧和充气轮胎、以及改进了的安全部件强化了这种基础设计。

---

rotate *v.* 旋转   pneumatic *adj.* 充气的

37

Indonesia's Minangkabau

The modern nation of Indonesia is an *archipelago* of 17,000 islands *clustered* around the equator, between the Indian and Pacific Oceans and the South China Sea. The climate is tropical, and geological instability can cause earthquakes and destructive tidal waves. A region rich with natural resources from spices to

印度尼西亚的米南卡保族

现代印度尼西亚，是由位于印度洋、太平洋和中国南海之间聚集在赤道周围的17 000多个小岛组成的岛国。热带气候和地质不稳定性会引起地震和破坏性浪潮。印度尼西亚，盛产香料和多种矿石，是一个自然资源极为丰富的地区，所以它一直是多种文化的十字交叉口。13

archipelago *n.* 群岛；列岛   cluster *v.* 结成群

minerals, Indonesia has been the crossroads of many cultures. The dominant religion on the islands was Hinduism until the rise of Islam in the thirteenth century. Colonized by the Dutch in the seventeenth century, Indonesia spent time under both British and Japanese rule and achieved independence in 1949.

Among the most distinctive of Indonesia's cultures is the Minangkabau group, which lives on the island of Sumatra. This is the largest *matrilineal* society in the modern world. (In a matrilineal society, descent is traced through the maternal, or mother's, line.) The Minangkabau follow a set of traditional practices called adat. Each family, for instance, has a rumah adat, or a "house for all adat." In this building, people related to each other through the mother's

---

世纪伊斯兰教崛起前，这个群岛的主流宗教是印度教。17世纪成为荷兰的殖民地后，印度尼西亚一直处在英国和日本两国的控制下，于1949年获得独立。

在印度尼西亚的文明中，最独特的是生活在苏门答腊岛的米南卡保族。这是现代世界最大的母系社会。（母系社会里，家族世系按母亲或母系血统追溯。）米南卡保人沿袭一套叫做"亚达特"的传统习俗。例如，每个家庭都有一座亚达特房屋，或称"容纳所有人的大房子"。母亲的家

---

mineral *n.* 矿物　　　　　　　　　　matrilineal *adj.* 母系的

family gather together to *rejoice* or sorrow, to make decisions or perform rituals.

Among the Minangkabau, the female line is called suku, and children take their mother's family name. Ancestral lands are passed down from mother to daughter. According to adat, a young man must wait for a marriage proposal from the families of eligible girls and on his wedding day is brought to the home of his bride. Also according to adat, a young man must leave his village to seek his fortune. Once a man has achieved financial success, he returns to his wife's village and her home. Although adat may be the normal way of life in the village, in the cities the Minangkabau tend to adopt a more traditional pattern.

族中相互有联系的人们聚集到这座建筑里庆祝或吊唁、制定决策或举行宗教仪式。

在米南卡保族，母系被称为"苏库"，且孩子们会随母姓。祖传的土地会由母亲传给女儿。根据亚达特，年轻男子必须等待中意的女孩家族的求婚，并且在结婚那天被带到他的新娘家里。同样，依照亚达特，年轻男子必须离开他的村庄去寻找发财之路，一旦赚了大钱，他得返回他妻子住的村庄和家。尽管亚达特可能是农村平常的生活方式，但是在城市里米南卡保人倾向于采取一种更传统的生活方式。

---

rejoice *v.* 欣喜

The name Minangkabau comes from an old David-and-Goliath-type story. A king on the nearby island of Java threatened to *invade*. Instead of a war, however, the groups staged a fight between two buffalo. The buffalo belonging to the Javanese was defeated; the other smaller one became known as the minang kabau, or "victorious buffalo." Buffalo fights are still popular entertainment for the Minangkabau. Each buffalo is linked by a rope to its owner, who *murmurs* quiet words, telling it how to fight. The contest, therefore, like the ancient battle against Java, is ultimately between the men and not the animals.

米南卡保这个名字由一个古老的大卫和歌利亚式的故事而来。临近爪哇岛的一个岛屿的国王扬言要入侵，然而，这些人安排了两头水牛来顶架，而不是进行一场战争。属于爪哇的那头水牛被打败了；另一头小一些的被称为米南卡保，即"胜利的水牛"。至今，斗水牛仍是米南卡保人喜欢的娱乐。每头水牛都由它们的主人用绳子牵着，主人会喃喃细语地告诉它们怎样顶架。所以，水牛顶架酷似他们古时候抵御爪哇人的战争，本质上是人与人而非动物与动物之间的拼杀较量。

---

invade *v.* 侵入   murmur *v.* 小声说

38

A Padang Feast

The foods of Indonesia are as varied as the societies that inhabit the islands of this tropical archipelago, and they reflect influences of centuries of trading partners and colonists. Today, the flavors of Indonesia come from *lemongrass*, hot chili paste called sambal, sweet coconut milk, acidic *tamarind* fruit, and pungent, gingery

巴东盛宴

如同生活在这个热带群岛的每个岛屿上的许多社会群体一样，印度尼西亚的食物多种多样，而且它们还反映了几个世纪以来贸易伙伴和殖民者带来的影响。今天，印尼人制作调味品所用原料有柠檬草、辣椒酱（亦称参巴酱）、甜椰奶、酸罗望子果和辛辣刺激的高良姜。

lemongrass *n.* 柠檬草   tamarind *n.* 罗望子果

galanga. The menu also includes a variety of fruits, including mangos and *papayas*.

One of the best-known Indonesian meals is an array of mostly spicy "fast food" items named after the West Sumatran capital of Padang. In a padang restaurant, the recipes are prepared in the morning and are then displayed for the diners' inspection. Ordering in a padang restaurant could not be any easier. Waiters bring each diner a large bowl of rice and a small bowl of water to use for handwashing. When the diner says the word makan, meaning "eat" or "I want to eat", the server returns with a great *assortment* of small dishes of fish, meat, and vegetables. Customers take small amounts of various items, experimenting with different sauces. The bland

---

菜单还有包括芒果和木瓜在内的多种水果。

印度尼西亚最有名的一道菜肴是一系列多半辛辣的"速食"食品，以西苏门答腊省省会巴东命名。在一家巴东餐馆里，食谱在早上就准备好，然后拿去给用餐者验对。在一家巴东餐馆点菜是再简单不过的事情。服务生会给每位用餐者端来一大碗米饭和一小碗用来洗手的水。当用餐者说了makan(音译：马坎)一词，意为"吃"或"我想吃饭"。服务生就会端过来一大份什锦小鱼配肉和蔬菜的套餐。用餐者应小量摄用每种食物，品尝

---

papaya *n.* 木瓜   assortment *n.* 花色品种

rice is the perfect vehicle for tasty (and often hot) delicacies—from *charcoal*-grilled chicken and fish curry to fried eggplant with chili sauce.

The traditional *beverage* that accompanies a padang meal is a glass of tea. A ripe banana makes a delicious dessert.

风格不一的调味汁。品尝诸如木炭烤鸡，咖喱鱼和辣椒油煎茄子等各类菜品时，最好辅以清淡的米饭。

　　巴东餐配用的传统饮料往往是一杯清茶，餐后甜点则是一根味甘可口的熟香蕉。

charcoal *n.* 木炭　　　　　　　　　　　　　　　　beverage *n.* 饮料

39

A Debate: The Impact of Prohibition

In the United States, the era known as Prohibition began when the Eighteenth Amendment to the Constitution went into effect in 1920. For the next 12 years, it was illegal to make, sell, or transport *intoxicating* beverages, defined as any drinks that were more than one half of one percent (0.5%) alcohol.

一场争论：禁酒令的影响

1920年，美国宪法第十八条修正案实施后，美国开始了史上闻名的禁酒时代。随后12年中，制作、出售或者运输经鉴定酒精含量超过0.5%的酒饮料，都属于违法行为。

---

intoxicating *adj.* 使人喝醉的

Prohibition came about largely because of the growth of the Temperance Movement. For almost a century, people had praised the virtues of *temperance*. These reformers believed that alcohol was the main cause of disease, broken homes, poverty, and crime. Many saw "demon rum" and "John Barleycorn" as enemies of a stable and productive world. By 1916 almost half of the 48 states had passed laws that closed saloons and *forbade* the production of any form of alcoholic beverage.

Prohibition, therefore, was an honest effort to improve the health of all Americans, to deal with the problems associated with excessive alcohol consumption, and to lower the cost of government intervention. Some historians suggest that Prohibition enjoyed widespread support and led to a drop in some forms of

---

很大程度上，禁酒令的颁布是由禁酒运动的发展所致。近一个世纪以来，人们一直赞扬自我克制的美德。改革者认为酒精是疾病、家庭破碎、贫穷和犯罪的主要诱因。许多人将"恶魔朗姆"和"大麦约翰"看为是稳定和高效生产世界之患。到1916年，几乎48个州中的半数通过了关闭酒吧和禁止生产任何种类的酒精饮料的法律。

由此看来，禁酒令，应对了与酗酒有关的一切问题，削减了政府的干预费用，是提高全体美国人健康状况的一次实实在在的努力。一些历史学家表明，禁酒令取得了广泛支持并减少了若干种犯罪。其他人反驳道，禁

---

temperance *n.* 禁酒；节制   forbid *v.* 禁止

crime. Others argue that it was the direct cause of increased crime, social conflict, and new forms of drug abuse. Whatever the case, the consumption of alcohol remained common throughout the United States despite the law.

It is hard to assess the impact of Prohibition. Bootlegging—the illegal manufacture and sale of liquor—was widespread and profitable, and *illicit* private clubs, called speakeasies, sprang up in place of the saloons that had been closed. The Customs Service and the Coast Guard struggled to *stem* the flood of alcohol coming in from places such as Canada and the Caribbean. The period also saw a drop in revenues for the government. Taxes could no longer be collected from the buyers and sellers of beer, wine, and spirits. Prison overcrowding was also a problem, partly because of

酒令是刑事犯罪增多、社会冲突和新毒品滥用的直接起因。无论怎样，尽管这项法令存在，酒品消费在美国仍然普遍。

禁酒令对美国有多大影响很难做出评价。贩私酒，即非法生产和出售酒类产品，确实波及范围广且有利可图。于是，一些非法私人俱乐部，亦称"地下酒吧"，突然泛滥成灾，取代了已关门停业的酒吧。海关总署和海岸防卫队竭力去遏制从加拿大和加勒比海等地涌入的私酒。这段时期，因无法从啤酒、红酒和白酒等各种经销商那里收缴到税金，政府税收也大幅减少。一定程度上，禁酒法令促成的监狱人满为患也构成了一个社会问题。

illicit *adj.* 违法的；不正当的   stem *v.* 阻止

violations of Prohibition laws.

Moreover, Prohibition-related crime quickly became organized. Individual criminals developed a network of relationships through which they could control *bootlegging* and provide protection to speakeasy owners. Corruption in police and government agencies also became a problem, as officers and civil servants were lured into a *lucrative* association with organized crime.

Prohibition ended in 1933 with the passage of the Twenty-first Amendment. The debate regarding its effectiveness continues to this day.

　　此外，与禁酒令有关的犯罪迅速演变为团伙犯罪。个体罪犯居然发展成一个既可控制私酒贩运又能为地下酒吧老板提供保护的巨大关系网。由于受利益诱惑，官员和公务员们跟犯罪团伙沆瀣一气，警务与政府部门的腐败现象也成为一种令人担忧的问题。

　　1933年，宪法第二十一条修正案获得通过，新法案终止了美国禁酒令，但关于禁酒令有效性的争论却一直持续到了今天。

---

bootleg *v.* 非法制造并出售　　　　　　　　　　lucrative *adj.* 获利丰厚的

40

Al Capone and Eliot Ness

Two familiar names from the era of Prohibition are Alphonse "Scarface" Capone and Eliot Ness. Theirs is the classic story of *flamboyant*, ruthless criminal and dogged, honest lawman.

Al Capone began his career in organized crime in Brooklyn, New York, where he earned his nickname. Capone's underworld

阿尔·卡彭和埃利奥特·内斯

禁酒时代出现了两个赫赫有名的人物："刀疤脸"阿尔·卡彭和埃利奥特·内斯。他们为人熟知是源于一个奢华、凶残的罪犯和一位坚毅、刚直不阿的执法者之间的传统故事。

阿尔·卡彭的团伙犯罪生涯始于纽约布鲁克林区。"刀疤脸"绰号也正是在这里得来的。然而，卡彭在黑社会发迹称霸，得从1919年依始他

---

flamboyant *adj.* 耀眼的；派头十足的

triumphs, however, belong mostly to his time in Chicago, Illinois, beginning in 1919. From there, he controlled a variety of illegal businesses, including *speakeasies* and gambling. It is thought that these businesses may have yielded as much as $100 million a year in profit. Capone was also the mastermind behind the St. Valentine's Day Massacre of 1929, in which seven members of a rival gang were executed.

Eliot Ness joined the U.S. Treasury Department in 1927. He was assigned to a leadership role in President Herbert Hoover's war on Capone's criminal empire. Ness and his investigators, later *dubbed* the Untouchables, gathered evidence of Capone's violations of Prohibition laws.

在伊利诺伊州芝加哥市混迹江湖阶段算起。在芝加哥，他控制着各种非法生意，其中包括地下酒吧和赌场。据估计，这些生意大约每年会给他带来近一亿美元的收益。卡彭还是1929年圣瓦伦丁节大屠杀的幕后操纵者。在这场屠杀中，敌对黑帮有7名成员死于非命。

1927年，埃利奥特·内斯入职美国财政部，被任命为赫伯特·胡佛总统专事打击卡彭犯罪帝国斗争的总指挥。内斯和调查员们，后来被人们戏谑为"不可接触者"，很快搜集到了卡彭及其团伙违反禁酒令的滔天罪证。

---

speakeasy *n.* 地下酒吧　　　　　　　　　dub *v.* 把……称为

Capone's men offered Ness *bribes*, but the attempt failed. In 1931 Capone was convicted of tax evasion. Sent first to the *penitentiary* in Atlanta, he was later transferred to Alcatraz prison in San Francisco. Capone, in poor health, was released from prison in 1939 and died in 1947. Ness died of a heart attack in 1957.

卡彭的手下向内斯行贿，但未果。1931年，卡彭被判逃税罪，先被押送到亚特兰大监狱，后又被转移到旧金山恶魔岛。1939年，卡彭刑满获释，因身体不佳，死于1947年。内斯于1957年死于心脏病突发。

bribe *n.* 贿赂

penitentiary *n.* 监狱

41

Suleiman I, the Magnificent

For almost 500 years, the Ottoman Empire was an essential *component* of trade, politics, and culture throughout the civilized world. The original Ottomans, Muslim Turks living in northwest Anatolia, helped to bring down the Christian Byzantine Empire, which had been in power for centuries. Eventually, the Ottomans

苏莱曼大帝

近五百年里, 奥斯曼帝国堪称整个文明世界贸易、政治和文化的核心部分。最早的奥斯曼人, 是住在阿纳托利亚的土耳其穆斯林, 他们帮助推翻了掌权几个世纪的基督教拜占庭帝国。最终, 奥斯曼人控制了从欧洲东南部和非洲北部到地中海东部边缘的大片区域, 还有从波

component *n.* 组成部分

controlled a huge region from southeastern Europe and northern Africa to the eastern edge of the Mediterranean Sea, as well as the Middle East from the Persian Gulf to the Black Sea.

Suleiman I, called "the Magnificent" or "the Lawgiver," ruled for 46 years in what has been described as a golden age. Born in 1494, he ascended the throne in 1520. His father, Selim I, nicknamed "Selim the Grim," had smoothed the way for Suleiman by *executing* all of his own brothers and nephews and four of his other sons.

Suleiman was *audacious* and brave. He fought at the head of his armies and was feared wherever he went. European forays into Asia and Africa posed a threat to his power and his own plans for

---

斯湾到黑海的中东地区。

被称为"苏莱曼大帝"或"立法者"的苏莱曼一世在位46年，他的统治时期被描述为一个黄金时代。他于1494年出生，1520年登上王位。他的父亲，绰号为"冷酷者塞利姆"的塞利姆一世，通过处死他所有的兄弟、侄子和他的其余四个儿子为苏莱曼铺平了道路。

苏莱曼，一身是胆，无所畏惧。他在战斗部队中一马当先，所到之处人人畏惧。欧洲人突袭亚洲和非洲对他的权力和扩张计划构成了威胁。作为应对之策，他利用各国之间的宿怨以及近期形成的宗教冲突，在假装与

---

execute *v.* 处死　　　　　　　　　　audacious *adj.* 大胆的

expansion. The strategy he devised in response exploited deep-seated hostilities between nations as well as new religious conflicts. He attacked the Catholic Holy Roman Empire in central Europe while forging an alliance with its enemy, the also-Catholic France. At the same time, he provided financial support to Protestant groups in northern countries fighting against Catholic lords. A Europe torn by religious and political *strife* found it hard to withstand his *assault*. Suleiman's armies, in fact, were not turned back until they virtually stood on the doorstep of Vienna, Austria.

Suleiman was also a man of creative vision and imagination. He made his capital city, Istanbul, the center of Islamic civilization—building mosques, palaces, bridges, and *aqueducts* that were as modern and magnificent as structures anywhere in the world. Suleiman was himself a poet and encouraged the work of painters, designers, musicians, writers, and philosophers.

敌国——当时也是以天主教为国教的法国，结成联盟后，向位于欧洲中心的天主教圣罗马帝国发动了进攻。同时，他为反对天主教贵族的北部国家新教团体提供经济援助，让宗教和政治冲突闹得四分五裂的欧洲难以挡住他的重兵来袭。事实上，苏莱曼大军直打到奥地利的维也纳城门处才无奈撤兵。

苏莱曼颇具创造力和想象力。他创建了自己的都城，伊斯兰文明的中心——伊斯坦布尔，建造了许多清真寺、宫殿、桥梁和沟渠，其现代化和壮观的程度堪于世界上任何建筑媲美。苏莱曼自己是一位诗人，并鼓励画家、设计师、音乐家、作家和哲学家进行创作。

---

strife *n.* 冲突　　　　　　　　　　　　　　　　　assault *n.* 袭击
aqueduct *n.* 沟渠

42

The Suleiman Mosque in Istanbul

A typical mosque includes a large central hall in which Muslims may gather, facing east toward the holy city of Mecca as they pray. A *minaret* or tower at the corner provides a place to sound the call to prayer. Many mosques include a madrasa, or school, with a library and a *residential* space for both teachers and

伊斯坦布尔的苏莱曼清真寺

每座典型的清真寺里面都有一个中央大厅。在大厅之内，穆斯林们集聚在一起面向东方朝拜麦加圣城。角落的宣礼塔为祷告的宣礼声提供了回荡的空间。许多清真寺都有一个穆斯林学校，为教师和学生提供一座图书馆和一处居所。

---

minaret *n.* （清真寺）宣礼塔，叫拜塔   residential *adj.* 住宅的

students.

Among the most magnificent mosques in the world is the Suleiman Mosque in Istanbul, Turkey. Founded by Suleiman I, it was constructed between 1551 and 1557. Its *architect*, Mimar Koca Sinan, designed hundreds of buildings for Suleiman; his father, Selim I; and his son, Selim II.

The complex of the Suleiman Mosque stands on a hill in an ancient quarter of the city. Four minarets, symbolic of Suleiman's role as the fourth Ottoman ruler over Istanbul, rise above the corners of a massive outer courtyard. Ten balconies on the minarets remind visitors that Suleiman was also the tenth *sultan* of the Ottoman dynasty. Inside the prayer hall, walls of pale marble support an enormous hemispherical dome that seems to rest on the light

---

　　世界上最宏伟的清真寺是位于土耳其伊斯坦布尔的苏莱曼清真寺。它是由苏莱曼一世创立，在1551和1557年间动工兴建。它的建筑师——科查·米马尔·希南为苏莱曼和他的父亲塞利姆一世以及他的儿子塞利姆二世设计了数百座建筑。

　　苏莱曼清真寺的建筑群坐落于这个城市山上的一个古建筑区。象征苏莱曼地位和伊斯坦布尔的第四位奥斯曼统治者的四座尖塔，高耸于一个巨大外部庭院的角落。尖塔的十个露台令参观者想起苏莱曼也是奥斯曼王朝的第十位苏丹。在祈祷大厅里，灰白色大理石墙面上装饰着巨大的穹顶，

---

architect *n.* 建筑师　　　　　　　　　　　　　　　　　　sultan *n.* 苏丹

streaming through the arched windows at its base. Additional windows, many of stained glass, *perforate* the walls in carefully designed patterns, creating dramatic contrasts of *illumination* and shadow and pools of color on the ground.

阳光透过拱形的窗子，洒在穹顶底部，墙面上还巧具匠心的设计了形状各异的窗子，窗子上嵌着带有花色的玻璃，阳光照射下形成强烈的对比，光线或明或暗、五彩斑斓。

perforate *v.* 在……上钻孔   illumination *n.* 照明

43

The Inca Trail

When the Spanish began colonizing South America in 1493, the Inca civilization of Peru was at its height. This empire high in the Andes Mountains boasted great cities and temple complexes, mountainside *terraces* used for farming, and a network of paved roads that connected even the most far-flung communities.

印加古道

1493年，当西班牙人开始把南美洲开拓为殖民地时，秘鲁的古印加文明正处于其最辉煌的时期。古印加帝国，位于安第斯山脉之中高海拔处，以其拥有大城市、寺庙建筑群、可耕用山坡梯田和甚至能连接到最遥远乡镇的铺面道路网而自豪。

---

terrace *n.* 梯田

The Inca Trail, which *incorporates* the remains of an old Inca roadway, begins near the ancient capital of Cusco and culminates in the dramatic ruins of Machu Picchu. It is a rugged hike about 27 miles long that takes most people four days to complete. The elevation is up to 13,779 feet above sea level. At this altitude, the air is very thin, and nausea and *fatigue* can be a problem for visitors.

Day 1 starts with a walk across the Kusichacha, or "bridge of happiness," that spans the Urubamba River. Among the ruins of ancient stone structures are villages where Incan descendents still grow corn and potatoes. Day 2 poses the greatest challenges as hikers move from the mild environment of forested valleys to

---

古风依存的印加古道，始于古都库斯科城边之地，终至令人瞩目的马丘比丘废墟。其总长度约为27英里，大部分人徒步旅行这一段崎岖古道需用四天时间。其海拔为13 779英尺，处于这样的海拔高度，空气一般非常稀薄，给游人带来最大的麻烦是晕眩和疲劳。

第一天，从步行横跨乌鲁班巴河上的"幸福桥"开始。这里的古石建筑遗迹中分布着一些村庄，古印加后裔仍然在这些村庄里种植玉米和马铃薯。第二天，对徒步旅行者来说，是最赋挑战性之旅，因为他们要从林木

---

incorporate *v.* 包含

fatigue *n.* 疲惫；疲乏

the Abra de Húarmihuamusa, or "dead woman's pass," high on the *treeless*, windy mountainside. Along the way on day 3, one can explore Sayaqmarka, or "town in a steep place," a *labyrinth* of halls reached by a stone stairway built into the edge of the mountain and an Inca tunnel dug some 66 feet through sold rock, and Phuyupatamarka, or "cloud-level town." On day 4, hikers enter Machu Picchu through Intipunku, or "gateway of the sun." Most buildings in Machu Picchu are one-room stone houses, once roofed with straw thatch, arranged around courtyards. There are a few larger structures whose purposes were probably religious. Terraces spill down the mountainsides all around.

After a challenging four-day trek, the best route home for many

覆盖的温和山谷地带辗转到一个寸木不生、狂风骤起的险峻山隘——"亡妇隘口"。 第三天，旅行者一路探险到"陡峭小镇"———重又一重过道组成的迷宫。到达这里先经过镶嵌在山边上的石头阶梯，再经过一条坚岩上凿出纵长约66英尺的称作"云层镇"的印加隧道。 第四天，徒步旅行者经"太阳之门"进入了马丘比丘。这里，大部分建筑为一室石屋，屋顶苫草，有一座围院。还有几座大一些的建筑，很可能是用于宗教活动的场所。山坡上到处都有向下排列的层层梯田。

四天富有挑战性的艰苦跋涉过后，对许多人来说回去的最好路线是乘

treeless *adj.* 无树木的   labyrinth *n.* 迷宫

will be the train that follows the *contours* of the Urubamba southeast back to Cusco.

History and the wonders of nature lure crowds of tourists to the Inca Trail. Both the ruins and the environment, however, have suffered from this *onslaught* of people. Trail erosion, the accumulation of garbage, and careless destruction of animal habitat and rare forms of plant life concern many people in Peru and around the world. Recently the government has increased fees and imposed stricter regulation on trash disposal in an effort to balance the benefits of tourism with the demands of historic preservation.

坐沿乌鲁班巴河东南岸回到库斯科的火车。

历史和自然奇观将成群的游客吸引至印加古道。然而，那里的遗迹和环境受到了严重人为损害。古道侵蚀、垃圾堆积以及对动物栖息地和稀有植物品种的粗心破坏引起了秘鲁和全世界人们的担忧。近年来，为了寻求旅游业效益和文物保护需求之间的平衡，政府增大了治改费用，并强制实行了更严格的垃圾管理制度。

---

contour *n.* 轮廓；等高线　　　　onslaught *n.* （常指难以应付的）大批；大量

44

The Nasca Lines

About 10 centuries before the Inca civilization in the Andes Mountains of Peru, the Nasca settled on the edges of the pampa—a vast, arid, stony plateau *devoid* of vegetation—on the south-central coast of that country. The Nasca occupied the area from about 200 B.C. to A.D. 600. When they disappeared, they left behind

纳斯卡线

在秘鲁安第斯山脉的印加文明形成1000年以前，纳斯卡人定居在潘帕——位于秘鲁中南海岸的一片广阔、荒芜、多石、缺乏植被的高原边缘。纳斯卡人从公元前200年到公元后600年间占据着这片区

---

devoid *adj.* 全无的

a mystery in the form of *geoglyphs*, or images engraved into the ground.

Most of these geoglyphs are geometric shapes such as straight lines, spirals, stars, and *trapezoids*. There are also naturalistic images of living things such as plants, birds, animals, sea creatures, and human beings. What is most remarkable is that these designs are so enormous that they are all but invisible to people on the ground.

Forgotten since the fifteenth century, the Nasca lines were noticed in the late 1920s by early aviators. At first it was thought that the lines formed some sort of astronomical calendar. Later theories

域。当他们消失后，留下了一片神秘的人工地貌，即刻入地中的图像。

这些人工地貌的多数都是直线形、螺旋形、星形和梯形的几何图形。还有一些植物、鸟类、动物、海洋生物和人类等生物的自然图像。最令人惊叹的是这些设计都庞大到地面上人的人几乎看不到。

自15世纪起纳斯卡线被人们遗忘了，直到20世纪20年代它们才被早期的飞行员注意到。最初，人们认为这些线组成了某种大文历法。后来理

geoglyph *n.* 地质印痕   trapezoid *n.* 不等边四边形

identified them as irrigation canals, sites of ceremonial practices, and roadways. Some people proposed that the lines had no purpose beyond artistic expression.

Research into these markings continues, as efforts are made to protect them from *malicious* and thoughtless abuse. In 1998 visitors and campers in the area damaged some of the lines, leaving behind garbage and tire tracks.

论证实它们是灌溉渠、举办仪式的场所和道路。有些人提出这些线除艺术表达外没有任何目的。

对这些标记的研究以及尽可能避免对它们蓄意和无意破坏的努力还在继续。1998年，来这个地区参观和宿营的人留下了垃圾和轮胎痕迹，毁坏了其中的一些线。

---

malicious *adj.* 恶意的